History of Haiti and its Revolution

History of Haiti and its Revolution

History and Civilization Collection

LM Publishers

Presentation

Haiti is an island in the West Indies. The actual republic occupies the western end of the island, and is separated from the Dominican republic by a line drawn from the river Pedernales on the south to the mouth of the river Massacre on the north. Its area is estimated at about 10,000 square miles.

It lies almost in the centre of the chain and, with the exception of Cuba, is the largest of the group.

The general history of the island begins with its discovery by Christopher Columbus, who landed from Cuba at Mole St Nicholas on December 1492. The natives called the country Haiti (i.e. mountainous country), and Quisquica (i.e. vast country); but Columbus named it Espagnola (Little Spain). It was inhabited by almost 2,000,000 Indians described as feeble in intellect and physically defective by the Spaniards. They were soon exterminated, and their place was supplied - as early as 1512 - by slaves imported from Africa.

The present capital of the island was founded six years after its discovery by Columbus.

About 1630, a mixed company of French and English, settled on the island of Tortuga, where they became formidable under the name of Buccaneers. They soon obtained a footing on the mainland of Haiti, and by the treaty of Ryswick, 1697, the part they occupied was ceded to France. This new colony, named Saint Dominique, subsequently attained a high degree of prosperity, and was in a flourishing state when the French Revolution broke out in 1789. The population was then composed of whites, free coloured people (mostly mulattoes) and negro slaves. The mulattoes demanded civil rights, up to that time enjoyed only by the whites; and in 1791 the National Convention conferred on them all the privileges of French citizens. The whites at once adopted the most violent measures, and petitioned the home government to reverse the decree, which was accordingly revoked.

In August 1791, the plantation slaves broke out into insurrection, and the mulattoes threw in their lot with them. A period of turmoil followed, lasting for several years, during which both parties were responsible for acts of the most revolting cruelty. Commissioners were sent out from France with full powers to settle the dispute, but although in 1793 they proclaimed the abolition of slavery, they could effect nothing. To add further to the troubles of the colony, it was invaded by a British force, which, in spite of the climate and the opposition of the colonists, succeeded in maintaining itself until driven out in 1798 by Toussaint Louverture. By treaty with Spain, in 1795, France had acquired the title to the entire island... (Encyclopedia Britannica, 1911)

General History of Haiti [1]

On August 3, 1492, Christopher Columbus left Palos. After a journey too well known to be repeated here, his three caravels anchored on December, 6, 1492, in a pretty bay in the northern part of Haiti. In honor of the saint whose feast the Catholic Church was celebrating that day, the place was called St. Nicholas. The beauty of the scenery, the lovely panorama which Columbus beheld on arriving, the song of the nightingale, the fish, everything reminded him of the country whence he started out to the conquest of the New World. Therefore he gave the name of Hispañola to the island he had just discovered; and believing that he was in Asia, he called the inhabitants "Indians." (Jacques N. Leger)

Adventurers from Europe, attracted chiefly by the exaggerated stories of gold, flocked thither, and the natives of the island were reduced to slavery, although many made a gallant resistance. After about 30 years of grinding servitude, nearly all the aborigines had disappeared. A few negroes were brought into the colony as early as 1505, and in

---

[1] Based on the work of John D. Champlin, junior.

1517 a royal edict authorized the importation from Africa of 4000 negroes a year. The blacks, stronger and better able to bear the labor which had been death to their predecessors, multiplied to such a degree that the island has finally passed into the hands of their descendants.

About 1630 a mixed colony of French and English, who had been driven out of St Christophers by the Spaniards, established themselves in the island of Tortuga, where they soon grew formidable under the name of buccaneers. They at last obtained a footing on the mainland of Haiti, into which they had previously made only predatory excursions; and by the treaty of Ryswick (1697) the part of the island which they held was ceded to France. The colony, called Saint Domingue, languished for a while under the restrictions imposed on its trade by the mother country, but after 1722, when these were removed, it attained a high degree of prosperity, and it was in a flourishing state when the French Revolution broke out in 1789.

The population was then composed of three classes, whites, free people of color (mostly mulattos), and slaves. The free people of color, some of whom were wealthy proprietors, demanded that the principles of the Revolution should be extended to them; this was opposed by the whites, who had previously engrossed all the public honors, and the two classes were already violently inflamed against each other when the national convention (1791) passed a decree giving to the mulattos all the rights of French citizens.

The whites adopted at once the most violent measures, and appealed to the mother country for a reversal of the decree. But when the mulattos took up arms for their defense at the time of the insurrection of the plantation slaves (August 23, 1791), the whites endeavored to conciliate them. In the meantime the home Government reversed the decree granting them political rights. The mulattos now took part with the blacks, and a most destructive war raged for several years, during which each party seemed to study to outdo the other in acts of cruelty. Commissioners were sent out from France, with full power to settle the quarrel, but could effect nothing.

In 1793 the abolition of slavery in the colony was proclaimed. In September of the same year a British force invaded the island; but, though some partial advantages were gained, the climate made sad havoc among the troops, and prevented any solid success. Toussaint Louverture, the leader of the blacks, came to the aid of the French, the home Government having in the meantime ratified the act of the commissioners in freeing the slaves. He was made commander-in-chief of the French army, and in 1798 forced the British to evacuate the island. By the treaty with Spain, made at Basel in 1795, France had acquired the title to the entire island, which now received the name of Saint Domingue.

In 1801 Toussaint, then master of the whole country, adopted a constitutional form of government, in which he was to be president for life. Bonaparte, then first consul of France, determined to reduce the colony and restore slavery, sent to Haiti 25,000 troops under General Leclerc. The blacks were compelled to retire to the mountains, but kept up a desultory war under Toussaint's able leadership. Leclerc, wearied of the war, cajoled the negro chiefs into a suspension of arms, and having invited Toussaint to an interview, seized him and sent him to France, where he died in prison in 1803. The blacks, infuriated by this act of treachery, renewed the struggle under Dessalines with a barbarity unequalled in the previous contests. The French, further embarrassed by the appearance of a British fleet off the coast, now gradually lost ground, and in 1803 agreed to evacuate the island. On the 30th of November of that year, 8000 French troops surrendered to the British squadron. In 1804 independence was declared, and the aboriginal name of Haiti was revived. Dessalines was made governor for life, but in October of the same year he proclaimed himself emperor, and was crowned with great pomp. He soon began to display the cruelty of a tyrant, and in 1806 he was assassinated. His position was now contended for by several chiefs, one of whom, Christophe, established himself in the north, while Pétion took possession of the southern part. The Spaniards re-established themselves in the eastern part of the island, retaining the French name, modified to Santo Domingo. Civil war now raged between the adherents of Christophe and Pétion, but in 1810 hostilities were suspended, Christophe declared himself king of Haiti under the title of Henry I.; but his cruelty caused an insurrection, and in 1820 he committed suicide. Pétion had died in 1818, and was succeeded by Gen. Boyer, who, after Christophe's death, made himself master of all the French part of the island.

In 1821 the eastern end of the island proclaimed its independence of Spain, and Boyer, taking advantage of dissensions there, invaded it, and in 1822 the dominion of the whole island fell into his hands. Boyer held the presidency of the new government, which was called the republic of Haiti, until 1843, when he was driven from the island by a revolution. In 1844 the people of the eastern end of the island again asserted their independence, and established the Dominican Republic, and from that date to the present time the two political divisions have been maintained; the Spanish made an effort to re-establish their authority in Santo Domingo by landing troops there in 1861, but withdrew in 1863. In Haiti several presidents rapidly succeeded each other, but in 1846 Soulouque, a black who had been a slave, was elected to the chief magistracy. He attempted to reconquer the eastern part of the island, but was defeated. In 1849 he assumed the title of Faustin I., emperor of Haiti, and in the following year was crowned. He was deposed in 1858, and a republic was proclaimed under the presidency of Fabre Geffrard, His administration was unpopular, and in 1867 he was obliged by an insurrection to abdicate and flee to Jamaica. He was succeeded in the presidency by Sylvestre Salnave. An insurrection broke out against him in 1868, and after a struggle of two years he was captured and shot. On May 29, 1870, Nissage-Saget was elected president, and Boisrond-Canal on July 17, 1876.

Haiti and its colonization[2]

I

Life in Haiti before its colonization

Jacques N. Leger wrote about Haiti that before the fifteenth century its inhabitants, numbering about one million, used to be relatively happy. They were very tawny, rather small in stature, with long, black, and smooth hair. Simple in their manners, more indolent than active, they were contented with little; moreover, their wants were not very great.

The men and the girls wore no clothing; the women only had around their waists a cloth reaching to their knees. They supported themselves by fishing, hunting, and by raising corn and vegetables of an easy culture; from their cotton they made nets, hammocks, etc.; they took great pleasure in smoking the dried leaves of the tobacco plant. Polygamy was practiced.

---

[2] Cf *Haiti: Her History and Her Detractors, by* Jacques Nicolas Léger.

Through the coarse ceremonies of their religion can be traced the idea of the immortality of the soul and the existence of a Supreme Being, whose mother, Mamona, was especially worshipped. In the life to come the good would be rewarded; and in their Paradise they would meet once more their relatives, their friends, and principally many women. They held sacred a cavern whence, according to their belief, the Sun and Moon escaped and went to shine in Heaven. Every year they celebrated in that grotto a kind of public feast; the "Cacique" or one of the notables headed the procession of men and women marching to the place. The ceremony began with the offerings that the priests or "butios" presented to the gods or Zemes, whilst the women danced and sang the praises of the deities. Afterward prayers for the salvation and prosperity of the people were said. Then the "butios" distributed among the heads of the families pieces of cake, which they preserved with great care; these consecrated cakes, according to a belief the vestiges of which can be found even up to the present among some civilized nations, had the virtue of warding off all dangers and diseases.

Their gods were strangely typified; they took the form of toads, turtles, snakes, alligators, and of hideous human faces. The "butios" were at once soothsayers and doctors. By tradition and through personal observation they knew the power of many plants; the simples helped them to make cures; and the art of healing increased their prestige.

The authority was divided between five military chiefs or "caciques," each one independent of the others. The weapons of the people consisted of clubs, arrows, and wooden spears the sharp ends of which were hardened by fire. Often they had to protect and defend themselves against the attacks of their insular neighbors, the Caribs (Caraibes), who were cannibals.

The people enjoyed dancing to the beating of a drum. There were no public or private festivities without such dancing and singing.

II

The arrival of the colonists

On those unfortunate people the arrival of the Spaniards was about to bring endless calamities. And the island up to that time so peaceful and quiet was to have no more tranquility; the land was to be nothing else than an everlasting battlefield, where all kinds of horrors and atrocities would be perpetrated. Torrents of blood would irrigate its fertile soil and a whole race would disappear in order to satisfy the cupidity of the newcomers. On the 12th of December, in setting up the cross on the coast of Haiti, Columbus had no idea that the symbol of redemption was to be the signal of a fierce struggle, of a struggle without mercy.

In fact, after the first impulse of curiosity caused by the sight of the large sails, which, like huge birds' wings, were carrying the caravels to their shore, the natives, prompted by the warnings of instinct, fled and got under shelter in the depths of their forests. The looks of the white men foreboded no good. But the trusting and kind disposition of the aborigines prevailed over fear. They were quickly won over by the cajoleries and the gifts of the Spaniards. Their leader, Guacanagaric, not only welcomed Columbus as a friend, but also became his ally; he granted the Admiral sufficient land for the building of a fortress. So a stronghold, called "The Nativity" in honor of that holy day, was erected with the help of the Indians not far from the place where the present town of Cap-Haitien is situated. The aborigines themselves had thus forged the first link of their own chains.

Thirty-nine men garrisoned the fortress, and on the 4th of January, 1493, Columbus left for Spain. He had scarcely set sail when the Spaniards, forgetting the simplest rules of prudence, became most unrestrained in their manners and committed the worst excesses. Taking no account of the generous hospitality and of the hearty welcome of Guacanagaric, they inflicted on his followers all kinds of ill treatment. They outraged women and girls, and despoiled the men of their goods. Eager for riches, and thinking only of acquiring gold, they seized the metal wherever they could lay their hands on it. They trampled on the chastity and the customs of the Indians. Finding no more booty in the "cacicat" of Marien, some of them decided to carry their depredations to the Maguana, where the auriferous mines of the Cibao were located. But Caonabo, the "cacique" of Maguana, was not like the passive Guacanagaric. Descending from the fierce tribe of the Caribs, he determined to remain the sole master of his "cacicat," which he had conquered by main force. Therefore he did not hesitate to cause the invaders to be arrested and put to death. And, having a vague presentiment of future perils, he determined to rid the island of the dangerous newcomers; in consequence he invaded the Marien. At the head of a numerous band of armed followers he rushed upon the fortress The Nativity, which he razed to the ground, after exterminating all the Spaniards. Henceforth it was to be war to the death.

When, on the 27th of November, 1493, Columbus returned to the place where The Nativity was built, he could but deplore the disaster. From Spain he had brought with him imposing forces. He settled in the eastern part of what is known to-day as Monte Christi; and there was built the first town erected by the Spaniards in the West Indies. In honor of the Queen of Spain this town was called Isabella.

Among Columbus's new companions there were many adventurers whose sole thought was to acquire riches. They began searching for gold with a greed second only to their contempt for the feelings of the Indians. Besides, the latter had to work hard to supply their oppressors with cotton, tobacco, and gold dust. They were soon compelled to fetch from the bowels of the earth that gold which in their indolence they had been content to pick up in the sands of the rivers. Their artless souls rose against such unjust oppression. They joined the party of Caonabo, who became the leader of the opposition to the tyranny of the foreigners. The natives fought gallantly. To get rid of his indomitable foe, Columbus had to resort to Alonzo Ojeda's perfidy. Under the pretext of making peace, they decoyed Caonabo into an ambush. As a gift from the chief of the Spaniards, Ojeda presented him with chains and handcuffs made of iron polished and glittering like silver. The unsuspecting Indian admired the irons, and mistaking them for ornaments he allowed himself to be manacled. He was then easily carried to Columbus, who kept him prisoner in his own house. Caonabo was afterward sent to Spain.

This treacherous act, instead of intimidating the Indians, provoked a general uprising. Manicatoex, Caonabo 's brother, became their leader. Against the band of numerous warriors who threatened the town of Isabella, Columbus despatched a well-disciplined body of foot-soldiers, cavalrymen, gunners, and arbolisters; twenty-five blood-hounds also were added to the army. In the struggle the natives fought desperately; but the firearms of the Spaniards prevailed over their spears and clubs. Their forces were annihilated. The cavalry harassed the fugitives, many of whom became the prey of the ferocious dogs. No quarter was granted, those only could escape who were lucky enough to reach the shelter of the inaccessible mountains. This victory secured the Spanish domination. The Indians agreed to pay tribute to them.

However, the tranquillity which followed these events did not last long; more terrible convulsions were in store for the unfortunate island.

The exactions of the Spaniards became unbearable. Hoping to get rid of them by starvation, the Indians gave up cultivating their lands; they deserted their homes, taking shelter in unsearchable forests in the mountains, where they lived on roots; they voluntarily endured hardships rather than submit to the treatment inflicted on them by the conquerors.

The Haitian soil was soon to be soaked with Spanish blood. In the absence of Columbus, who left for Spain in 1496, his companions quarreled and civil war began. On all sides bloody scenes were enacted: the Spaniards exterminating the Indians; the latter availing themselves of the least opportunity to retaliate; and to crown the situation, the Spaniards killing each other.

On his return to Hispañola, Columbus suppressed the dissensions among his followers by establishing, in behalf of Roldan-Jimenes, the leader of the malcontents, what is known as the "repartimientos" system: he granted to Roldan and to his followers a certain quantity of land and a sufficient number of Indians to cultivate it. In that manner slavery began to appear; and Quisqueya had a new horror to add to the list of the calamities with which its unhappy inhabitants were already afflicted.

In 1500 Bobadilla succeeded Columbus; and the "repartimientos" system became worse. The "caciques" were compelled to supply every Spaniard with a certain number of Indians; these Indians were made to work under the guidance and in behalf of their masters, to whose heirs they were transferable.

Naturally this caused the natives to be still more highly displeased. Moved by their complaints the court of Spain appointed Nicholas Ovando governor of the island; he landed in Santo Domingo on the 15th of April, 1502.

The new governor had a good reputation, which he soon belied. It would seem that in reaching Hispañola the best-intentioned man laid aside his kind disposition to give way to his worst instincts. Thinking only of shipping as much gold as possible, in order to convince the King of Spain of the merit of his administration, Ovando was pitiless to the Indians. These unfortunate people, accustomed to the sunshine, were made to live in the depths of the earth; and many of them died from starvation and exhaustion.

From the Canary Islands Pierre d'Atença brought the sugar-cane to Hispañola. This new culture increased the burden which was already so heavy for the natives.

With a view to preventing any uprising on their part Ovando decided to destroy the last centres of organization where they could gather their forces for a common resistance. On his arrival two of the former "cacicats" were still holding their own and recognized the authority of two aborigines.

Anacaona, widow of the gallant Caonabo, governed the Xaragua, and the Higuey was ruled by Cotubanama. The prestige of the Queen of Xaragua was very great. She was a beautiful woman, possessing the art of lulling away the cares of her people by extemporizing for them the naive songs they were so fond of. Like her husband, Anacaona was to be a victim of the Spanish tyranny. Ovando took umbrage at the moral ascendency she possessed over the natives. Under the pretext of collecting the tribute due to the Court of Spain, he left for the Xaragua, escorted by 300 foot soldiers and 70 cavalrymen. In pursuance of instructions given by Anacaona, the people everywhere gave him the most friendly welcome. The Queen herself went to meet her illustrious visitor, in honor of whom many festivities took place.

But all this confidence did not move the inexorable Spaniard. During one of the festivities, at a given signal agreed on beforehand, Ovando's soldiers rushed upon the harmless Indians and began a wholesale slaughter. They set fire to the village, thus rendering the massacre still more horrible. Anacaona, now a prisoner, was dragged away to Santo Domingo, where a mock court of justice, completing Ovando's treachery, sentenced her to death. Neither her beauty nor her charms could excite the compassion of the conquerors, and she was hanged. Thereafter Ovando was master of the Xaragua. (1504.)

But the Higuey was still under the authority of the stalwart Cotubanama. It was an easy matter to find a pretext for waging war on him. The last of the Haitian "caciques" defended his small State with great bravery. The struggle was a fierce one. The Spanish fury spared neither sex nor age. They massacred the natives indiscriminately. Vanquished at last, Cotubanama was taken as a prisoner to Santo Domingo where, like Anacaona, he was hanged. Through his defeat and death the Spaniards at last acquired the entire possession of Hispañola.

Ovando was victorious. The Spanish conquest had annihilated a whole race. Shipped to Europe and sold as slaves, heavily burdened with taxes, over-worked, tormented, persecuted, the autochthons had rapidly disappeared. Many had resorted to suicide to escape from the ill treatment inflicted on them; others were devoured by the ferocious dogs; the greatest number had fallen in the bloody wars and bloody massacres. In 1507, scarcely fifteen years after the arrival of the Spaniards, there remained, out of a population numbering about 1,000,000, only 60,000 natives. Four years later, in 1511, these 60,000 were reduced to 14,000.

The cruelty and cupidity of the newcomers had depopulated the island. There was in consequence a great deficiency of laborers: the prosperity of Hispañola was in jeopardy. Ovando, always fruitful in expedients, conceived the idea of importing the inhabitants of the neighboring islands, pretending that it would be easier to convert them to Christianity. Deceived by the grossest artifices, 40,000 of those unfortunate people were removed from their homes and became at Hispañola the prey of the Spanish avidity.

The Spaniards soon introduced into the island a new element more resisting than the Indians and Caribs: a few blacks had been sold in the colony. Pleased with their work, the Spaniards held the Africans as indispensable. The slave-trade which ensued was the cause of the downfall of the colonists. Cargoes of human flesh abounded in Hispañola. Stunned by their brutal separation from their families, stupefied by the sufferings and the fatigues of a long journey, scattered on the various plantations, and unable to understand the language spoken around them, the new slaves were at first necessarily docile and obedient. But, little by little, through contact with the survivors of the last Indians, they began to be able to exchange ideas among themselves. And the old grievances uniting with the new ones served to augment the hatred of the oppressors.

In 1519 occurred the last uprising of what was left of the first inhabitants of the island. Saved almost miraculously from the massacre of Anacaona's followers in 1504, Henri, a native of Bahoruco, was taken to Santo Domingo and brought up in a convent of Dominican friars. Though he became a Christian, he was nevertheless a slave. Tired of all the ill treatment inflicted on him by his master, incensed by an attempt on his wife's honor, and being unable to obtain justice, he fled in 1519; accompanied only by a few Indian slaves who swore to die rather than endure again the humiliation of their former condition, he took refuge in the mountains of Bahoruco.

This new leader could read and write; and like some of his companions he understood the use of firearms. They could therefore successfully hold their own. The Spanish pride received blow after blow. Henri's victories encouraged all the Indians who could make their escape to flock to his camp.

The black slaves were not long in following the example of their companions in misfortune. They rebelled on the very plantation of Diego Columbus, governor of the island. They set fire to all the farms they found on their way and killed every European they met. But, being without a leader and having only a slight knowledge of the country, they met with rapid defeat. Yet many of them were fortunate enough to reach the Ocao Mountains, where there lived already some men of their race, known as maroons, who had freed themselves from slavery.

The Spaniards failed to subdue Henri either by force or by deceit. He firmly established his authority in the Bahoruco, and his followers became the terror of the colonists. It was now his turn to inflict humiliations on the conquerors; which he did for more than fourteen years. The frequent defeats met by the Spaniards decided Charles V, then King of Spain and Emperor of Germany, to send a special agent to Hispañola: Barrio-Nuevo was intrusted with the mission of restoring peace. Bearing a letter from the Emperor to Don Henri, he had no trouble in persuading the "cacique" to lay down his arms. Acting by the advice of Las Cases, who was called the "Protector of the Indians," Henri went to Santo Domingo. A solemn treaty of peace was made and ratified on both sides. Henri was allowed to reside in the village of Boya. Exempt from paying tribute, he was to be called "cacique of Haiti" and to keep under his command the Indians who were permitted to follow him. These, numbering about 4,000, the last scions of the aboriginal race, settled at Boya.

They had at last recovered their liberty. Henceforth they would be able to lead a quiet life.

III

The French conquest

The treaty signed in 1533 with the "cacique" Henri had at last put an end to the hostilities between the Indians and Spaniards. For a while there was no bloodshed. The relative tranquillity which ensued was not taken advantage of. Instead of thriving, the colony was on the wane. The incompetency or malversation of the various governors hastened the decline. The mines were emptied or deserted; no care was given to agriculture. In consequence, through idleness, debauchery and poverty the colonists were in a piteous condition. Everything was falling to ruin. The town of Santo Domingo alone, where was centred the luxury of the administrators, remained prosperous and assumed the appearance of great splendor. But its magnificence was the cause of serious calamities. In 1586 the English admiral, Sir Francis Drake, charged by Queen Elizabeth to curb the Spanish arrogance, bombarded the town, took possession of it, and partly destroyed it by fire. After an occupation of a month he agreed to evacuate it in consideration of a ransom of £7,000.

The arrival of other Europeans in the West Indies was to become a source of continual worry to the Spaniards. From the beginning of the sixteenth century, attracted by the allurements of gain, the French had begun making incursions into the New World. Impressed by the various tales concerning the riches of Santo Domingo city, they little by little commenced the habit of calling the whole island Saint-Domingue. At first they had no idea of conquest. They were satisfied with plundering. In concert with the English they lost no opportunity of injuring the Spanish trade. However, successive defeats made them feel the necessity of having a rallying-point, at least a place where they could refit their ships. In 1625 a party of Frenchmen under the command of Enembuc, and of Englishmen, under the leadership of Warner, took possession of St. Christopher Island. Private initiative began thus to deprive Spain of its possessions in the West Indies.

The presence of these dangerous neighbors alarmed the Court at Madrid. In 1630 Admiral Frederic de Tolède expelled both the English and French from St. Christopher. Looking for a safer shelter, they settled at Tortuga Island (La Tortue), situated in the northern part of Hispañola or Saint-

Domingue. Their new possession, eight leagues long and two leagues wide, became rapidly the rendezvous of the freebooters who swept the Spanish Main. In 1640 the French drove the English from this small island, thus remaining the sole masters. That was the starting point of their settlement in Saint-Domingue.

At that time the Spanish colony was in full decline. Owing to the necessity of preserving themselves from the depredations of their terrible foes, the Spaniards had almost deserted the coasts and were concentrated in the interior of the island. The Frenchmen availed themselves of the opportunity to take possession of the greatest part of the northern seashore. They had Port Margot, and soon founded Port-de-Paix.

These new inhabitants of Saint-Domingue were rough men of very coarse manners. They devoted their time to hunting wild oxen, the flesh of which they dried and smoked over a wood-fire called "boucan"; hence their name of buccaneers. But hard pushed by the Spaniards they turned their attention to piracy, tinder the name of freebooters they were the terror of the West Indies. They had neither wives nor families. They entered two by two into a kind of partnership, all of whose goods were in common and to be inherited by the survivor. In case of a disagreement, which seldom happened however, blood alone could bring the quarrel to a close. Even in their dress they were wild looking. At their belts could always be seen a sabre, besides several knives and daggers. Any one of them possessing a good gun and twenty -five hunting-dogs considered himself a happy man. Many abandoned their family names and assumed pseudonyms, which remained to their descendants. Continually exposed to the inclemencies of the weather, their lives in constant jeopardy, they had as little fear of death as regard for the laws. They were fierce and desperate in their bravery; they roamed the seas in their small crafts, and would board fearlessly the largest Spanish ships. Nothing could resist the impetuosity of their attacks. The independence of their nature tolerated no restraint; and the authority of their leaders lasted only so long as fighting was going on. Improvident and careless, they would squander in a few days the valuable booty they acquired, their lives being thus continually spent either in the greatest luxury or in the utmost poverty. Want therefore excited their ardor and aroused their courage.

D'Ogeron undertook to discipline these unruly spirits and to interest them in the welfare of their new country. He thought that family ties alone could check their wild dispositions and bind them to their homes. So he requested that some women be sent from the mother country; at first but few arrived. Therefore, to prevent any quarrelling, they were awarded to the highest bidders; the less destitute among the freebooters were thus able to secure female companions. In this manner the first French families were instituted in Saint-Domingue.

The freebooters were not to be trifled with; they were terrible foes. The Spaniards made vain efforts to exterminate them. A new and relentless war began; the island once more became a battlefield. The English thought they had now a good opportunity to take possession of the country. A fleet sent by Cromwell threatened Santo Domingo in 1655. Fortunately for the French the expedition failed and the English proceeded to Jamaica, which they seized, thus depriving Spain forever of that colony. The struggle at Saint-Domingue continued therefore between the French and the Spaniards only; it was a stubborn and bloody contest. The French not only held their own, but even managed to gain a surer footing.

Emboldened by their success they now assumed the offensive; they desired the entire possession of the island. In their first campaign against Santiago they stormed the city, which they afterward abandoned upon receiving a ransom (1669).

At the first opportunity the Spaniards retaliated. They invaded Petit-Goave, which they completely destroyed. In 1691 they took possession of Cap-Français, which they set on fire and whose inhabitants they massacred. On leaving the ruined city they took with them a great number of women, children, and slaves. The French for a while were in a desperate state. Besides the Spaniards, the English also were threatening their settlement. And the black slaves, whose hope of liberty was only slumbering, began to cause some anxiety. In 1678 Padrejean had roused them to rebellion. In 1697, in the Quartier-Morin, 300 Africans took up arms again.

Fortunately for the French the timely peace of Riswick put an end to the hostilities. By the treaty signed in 1697 Louis XIV acquired a clear title to the possession of the western part of the island, the limits of which were established from Cap-Rose in the north to La Beate in the south.

IV

Changes on the island

By recognizing the French conquest the treaty of Riswick rid the colonists of Saint-Domingue of their anxieties arising from the vicinity of the

Spaniards. The latter even became their allies, the war for the succession of the throne of Spain having just confounded the interests of Louis XIV with those of the heir of Charles II.

The eighteenth century began under the happiest auspices; quiet once established, Saint-Domingue was not long in astonishing the world by its prosperity. The ardent tropical heat, however, soon exhausted the vigor of the hired Europeans known as "engagés," whose position resembled that of serfs. The cultivation of sugar-cane and of indigo required hardier constitutions. In consequence the Africans were in favor. Nobody hesitated to participate in the slave-trade. As many as 30,000 blacks were annually imported.

In the beginning their position, pitiable as it seemed, was less hard to bear. The first colonists, unsociable and haughty, had however very simple tastes. Their wants up to that time were not numerous and were easily satisfied. In the colony there was a scarcity of white women, and those who had arrived about the beginning of the French occupancy could not be regarded as models of austere virtue. The fierce free-booters and their immediate successors did not consider the negresses as unworthy of their attentions. The unbounded devotion of the latter often moved the hearts of the terrible masters whose companions they had become. The children born of such a commerce were not entirely neglected by their fathers. There existed no color prejudice to complicate the relations of the two races. No one had cause to feel shame or humiliation. The appearance of the mulatto, in arousing feelings of fatherly love, ameliorated the condition of some of the slaves. Mothers and children were often freed owing to these sentiments. Unfortunately through the riches resulting from the fruitful soil of Saint-Domingue these ideas began to suffer a change. Surrounded by extravagant luxury, the wealthy colonists made it the fashion to look down upon the Africans and their descendants. And the new families, arrived from Europe, exaggerating this disdain, hardly considered as human beings those whose color was not white. Barriers arose; and the odious distinctions between men, which the Gospel was supposed to have done away with, were more than ever firmly established.

At the time of its greatest splendor the inhabitants of Saint-Domingue were divided into three distinct classes: the whites, the "affranchis" or freedmen, and the slaves. To these classes officially admitted, may be added a fourth one—the maroons.

Naturally the whites had arrogated all the privileges. They were the masters; their color sufficed to confer on them all the rights and advantages. However, interest and prosperity in time divided the predominant class, introducing four subdivisions: 1st, civil and military functionaries; 2nd, the wealthy planters; 3rd, merchants; 4th, mechanics, storekeepers and adventurers in quest of success. These groups were jealous of one another. And those who were neither functionaries nor wealthy planters were scornfully called "petits blancs." The latter were envious of the social position of the former. Besides, the white natives of Europe considered themselves far above the Creoles, *i. e.*, those who were born in the colony.

Notwithstanding these distinctions prompted by their unbearable vanity, all of them—the whites from Europe, Creoles, wealthy planters, and "petits blancs"—made common cause in the matter of taking advantage of the colonial régime which allowed them to trample upon the slaves, and to heap humiliations upon the "affranchis." However, the wealthy planters, who formed the aristocracy of the island, could not disguise their displeasure at the despotic and military government of Saint-Domingue.

The Governor-General had usurped supreme power. He interfered with everything, even in the administration of justice, thus usurping the duties of a special agent or "intendant" who was there for that purpose. His word was supreme law.

The wealthy planters thought that the surest way for their party to become the ruling power was by shaking off his authority. Hence a bitter rivalry, and an underhand war began between them and the Governor-General.

While undermining the position of the agents appointed by the King of France, the planters did nothing to gain the sympathy of the "petits blancs"; and their contempt for the "affranchis" was too great to allow them even to think of them as allies.

The "affranchis" formed the intermediary class between the colonist and the slave, and consisted of the blacks and mulattoes who had been able to obtain or to buy their freedom. Through personal efforts and hard work they began to rise gradually from the low condition they had occupied from their birth. They acquired urban and rural property; they appreciated learning; and their sons, sent to France at great sacrifice to themselves, had often more success at school than the children of the colonists.

The wealth and knowledge they acquired made the "affranchis" feel they were the equals of the whites. Therefore they were highly indignant over the prerogatives the latter had assumed at their expense. They claimed the exercise of the political rights granted them by the Black Code. Circumstances placed them face to face with the colonists, who sought to check their ambition by humiliating them. Thus the liberal professions were closed to the "affranchis"; they were debarred from learning any kind of trade; they could not be silversmiths, for instance. In the army they could no longer become officers. At last they were even forbidden to go to France (1777); and were ordered to wear clothes of a material different from the whites.

And yet those men upon whom the colonists heaped humiliation after humiliation were good soldiers. They were enlisted in both the militia and the horse-police (maréchausée); and they all understood the use of firearms. It was into the hands of such men that the colonists committed their safety. As a means of putting a stop to the ever-increasing colonial pride and haughtiness, the women, mulattresses and blacks alike, resorted to their native charms. Wives or concubines, they availed themselves of whatever influence they possessed to secure the freedom of the men of their race. Incensed by the preference shown to their colored sisters, the white women added the weight of their jealousy to the already existing causes of conflict.

The slaves were in a pitiable plight. Not being considered as human beings, they were entirely without rights that a white man was bound to respect. They were treated and sold like cattle, with which their masters confounded them in the inventory of their estates. They were subjected to the most barbarous punishments. According to the Black Code all fugitives were punishable by death; it was lawful to mutilate them by chopping off their legs and their ears. The hounds were let loose on them, inflicting the greatest torture by their fierce attacks on the unfortunate creatures. Flogging was the mildest chastisement inflicted on the slaves. The honor of their wives, the chastity of their daughters were matters of the slightest consideration to their masters.

Small wonder it was that the slave was beset with one fixed idea—to free himself of that odious yoke. Throughout his sufferings he never despaired: liberty was the one hope of his existence. And when he could not buy his freedom he would secure it for himself by fleeing; at the first opportunity he would fly for safety into the densest forests and the most inaccessible gorges of the mountains. When he was successful in effecting his escape he became what was called a maroon.

Hence the maroons were slaves who, at the risk of their lives and after undergoing untold hardships, had eventually recovered their freedom. Being outlaws and hunted like wild animals they had continually to be on the lookout. Any place where they could find a safe shelter from their pursuers became their domain. Should they happen to be caught by their owners they knew beforehand that no mercy was to be expected and that the most inhuman punishments the colonial imagination could invent would be theirs. Consequently, when attacked they fought with the fiercest desperation. Theirs was a perpetual struggle for existence. It was these men, without education or culture, who gathered from their confused ideas of human dignity the necessary energy to wage war on the society which was oppressing them so brutally. The first to bid defiance to the colonial system, they showed the men of their race that hardships, sufferings, even death—all were preferable to such degrading servitude. They formed the vanguard of the future army of liberation.

Such were the four classes of men who inhabited Saint-Domingue; the clashing of whose conflicting aspirations was destined to hurl them one against the other. After irrigating the Haitian soil with their sweat, "affranchis," slaves, and maroons firmly united, would lavish their blood on it in order to root out forever the shameful institution of slavery.

V

The slaves and the "affranchis"

In 1789 there were at Saint-Domingue 520,000 inhabitants, 40,000 of whom were white, 28,000 "affranchis," and 452,000 slaves. The number of maroons was from two to three thousand. Whilst most of the whites led corrupt and dissolute lives, the "affranchis," through domestic virtues, were acquiring much wealth; they possessed a third of the real estate, and a fourth of the personal property of the colony. Yet no regard was shown them. Despite the levelling and philanthropic philosophy which in Europe was moving the heart of the nobility, the colonists became daily more and more haughty and overbearing to the men of the black race; they did all in their power to check the hopes which these new ideas began to raise in the souls of the sorely oppressed slaves.

Through their influence and intrigues the colonists extorted from the weak hands of Louis XVI decisions of the most insulting nature against the "affranchis." The excess of humiliations heaped on them at last moved, even in France, the pity of generous hearts. "La Société des Amis des Noirs" soon extended its mighty support to the lawful claims of those who hitherto were treated like pariahs.

The "affranchis" became more and more conscious of their importance. In 1779, responding to the call of the Comte d'Estaing, 800 blacks and mulattoes left their families and their homes, and went to fight side by side with the soldiers of George Washington. At the siege of Savannah the colored sons of Haiti fearlessly shed their blood for the independence of the United States. After fighting for the liberty of others was it possible that they would willingly tolerate slavery for their mothers, their brothers, and their sisters? Could they be content under the arbitrary rule of a system which had despoiled them of their rights?

But, blinded by their prejudice, the wealthy planters would not make the slightest concession in their favor. They founded in Paris the "Club Massiac," which became henceforth the centre of action of their coterie. Yet at that time the pretensions of the "affranchis" were very moderate. What was it they were claiming? Simply the equality of political rights which was granted to them in 1685 by the Black Code.

By yielding to their requests the colonists would have saved their property, and Saint-Domingue might perhaps have remained a part of the French territory. Still they chose to run the greatest risks rather than share the administration of the island with men whom they considered their inferiors.

From the convocation of the States General, the wealthy planters began to defy the colonial authority, thus giving the first example of insubordination. On their own responsibility they secretly appointed eighteen representatives whom they sent to France. On their arrival at Versailles they found the National Assembly already organized. This first act of insubordination was followed by others still more important. When the news of the fall of the Bastille reached Saint-Domingue, the pretensions of the colonists knew no bounds. They elected municipalities and even an Assembly, which, assuming the title of "General Assembly of the French part of Saint-Domingue," met at Saint-Marc and arrogated full powers. On the 28th of May, 1790, this Assembly adopted a decree which constituted almost a declaration of independence. The attitude and encroachment of this body was naturally highly displeasing to the colonial government, which ordered its dissolution and resorted to force in order to compel its members to disperse. The whites took no pains to conceal from the "affranchis" the discord existing among themselves.

Excluded from all the assemblies elected at Saint-Domingue, the freedmen had never ceased to protest against the arbitrary deprivation of their political rights. Their representatives in France, among whom were Julien Raymond and Vincent Ogé, were fighting hard to put an end to their humiliating position. Through the powerful assistance of the Society "des Amis des Noirs," they were received, on the 22d of October, 1789, by the National Assembly. Later on the "affranchis" offered to France 6,000,000 francs and the fifth of their properties in guarantee of the national indebtedness. The Assembly was not long in taking up the slavery question. Whilst the matter was under discussion, Charles de Lameth, one of the wealthy planters, spoke, on the 4th of December, in favor of the freedom of the blacks and claimed their right to become members of the colonial assemblies.

The colonists decided that the time had come to check the audacity of the "affranchis," and as usual they resorted to all kinds of atrocities. In the town of Cap-Français the mulatto Lacombe was hanged, his only crime having been that he dared to present a humble petition claiming the "Rights of man" (Les Droits de l'homme). At Petit-Goave, a highly respected old man, Fernand de Baudières, a white, was beheaded. He was charged with having drawn up a petition asking, not for equality of rights in favor of the "affranchis," but only for a slight betterment of their condition. At Aquin, a mulatto, G. Labadie, seventy years old, simply suspected of having in his possession a copy of the petition, was attacked by night at his home by the whites. Severely wounded, this septuagenarian, a man universally esteemed, was tied to the tail of a horse and dragged through the streets. At Plaisance, the mulatto Atrel, guilty of having accepted a claim upon a white man, was killed by a band of infuriated people. At Fonds-Parisien the whites set fire to the most important sugar refineries of the "affranchis" Desmares, Poisson, Renaud. In time to come, the slaves who revolted, remembering this merciless destruction of property, in their turn reduced to ashes the rich plantations of the colonists.

The French spared not even the children. At Petite-Rivière de l'Artibonite a party of 25 whites, after searching in vain for a mulatto, ended by killing his two children; in the same locality they murdered a father and his two sons. A black freedman was, without the least provocation, put to death by a party of whites; whilst at Cap-Français there took place a wholesale slaughter of the "affranchis" by the colonists. Such are the atrocities with which the wealthy planters started the French revolution in Saint-Domingue. By and by both "affranchis" and slaves retaliated by taking revenge of all the horrible crimes of which they had been the victims. Many foreign writers unfriendly toward

Haiti make mention only of the reprisals; but they intentionally omit all allusion to the frequent revolting crimes which had caused them.

By a decree of March 8, 1790, the National Assembly had, however, indicated the powers vested in the colonial assemblies of the French possessions. And, according to article 4 of the Instructions adopted on the 28th of the same month, all persons 25 years old, owning real estate or domiciled in the parish for two years and paying taxes, were authorized to take part in the election of those assemblies. The "affranchis" possessed the full requirements, and therefore imagined that they would at last be able to exercise their political rights. Their illusions did not last long. The colonists of Saint-Domingue did not consider as *persons* men of the black race; they regarded them as *things*. In consequence they were not allowed to vote.

Foreseeing the decision of the wealthy planters, Vincent Ogé, one of the commissioners of the "affranchis," decided to return to Saint-Domingue in order to demand the fair application of the Decree and the Instructions of March, 1790. He assumed the pseudonym of Poissac; and in spite of all the hindrances placed in his way he succeeded in leaving France. He arrived at Cap-Français in the evening of October 16, 1790, and proceeded forthwith to Dondon, his native place. As soon as his arrival became known the colonists took the necessary steps to secure his arrest. From Dondon Ogé went to Grande-Rivière to the house of Jean-Baptiste Chavanne. Of a practical mind, Chavanne was firmly convinced that nothing would be obtained from the whites by persuasion only. He therefore advised an immediate uprising of the slaves. Ogé deemed this plan too radical. In consequence, on October 21, he wrote to Count Peinier, then Governor of the island, saying that he had come to secure the application of the Decree of March, 1790, and that, in order to put an end to an unjust and absurd prejudice, he would, in case of need, repel force by force. As a result of this step, and in spite of his threat, a price was set upon his head, and 800 soldiers were despatched against him. Ogé had only 250 followers. The first encounter was favorable to him. But new forces sent from Cap-Français defeated his small army. He succeeded, with Chavanne and a few companions, in reaching the Spanish part of the island. The Governor, Don Joachim Garcia, had the cruelty to give them up to the government of Saint-Domingue. After a so-called trial, Ogé and Chavanne, to whom even the assistance of a lawyer was denied, were sentenced "whilst alive to have their arms, legs, thighs and spines broken; and afterward to be placed on a wheel, their faces toward Heaven, and there to stay as long as it would please God to preserve their lives; and when dead, their heads were to be cut off and exposed on poles, Vincent Ogé's on the highway leading to Dondon, and Chavanne's on the road to La Grande Rivière, opposite the estate of Poisson." This barbarous sentence was executed in all its horror on February 25, 1791. The northern provincial assembly gathered together in state to witness this inhuman punishment. Ogé and Chavanne, hacked to death, bore their sufferings stoically. For many months following, their unfortunate companions were hunted and when caught were hanged. The method employed for quelling the insurrection was savage and merciless. But the revenge soon to be taken equalled in mercilessness the acts which provoked it. Before the end of 1791 the colonists were to begin to expiate their crimes.

Remaining still haughty and full of pride they imagined that the martyrdom of Ogé and Chavanne would so intimidate the "affranchis" that they would not dare to renew the struggle. As a matter of fact, after Ogé's defeat, the free blacks and mulattoes of the South, who, under the leadership of André Rigaud, had gathered on the plantation of Prou, willingly laid down their arms. But this proved to be only a truce. The colored men wanted time in which to form and to mature their plans. Ogé's fate made it clear to them that by force alone they would conquer the power of exercising the political rights which they had vainly endeavored to acquire peacefully.

Tranquilized by their recent victory and the apparent submission of the "affranchis," the wealthy planters began to renew their intrigues against the colonial government. Two battalions, sent from France with a view to helping to maintain order in Saint-Domingue, arrived at Port-au-Prince on March 2, 1791. The friends of the former Colonial Assembly of Saint-Marc, which had been severely arraigned by the National Assembly in a resolution adopted on October 12, 1790, won over the soldiers to their cause. The latter landed in Port-au-Prince in disobedience to the orders given them by the Governor-General, Mr. de Blanchelande. The city was in open rebellion. The prison was stormed. André Rigaud, Pinchinat, and some other "affranchis" who were then in jail were set free. Mr. de Blanchelande left hastily for Cap-Français. The colonists murdered Colonel Mauduit, whose fidelity to the colonial government had displeased them; his body was mutilated and his head, stuck on the end of a pole, was carried through the streets of Port-au-Prince. They usurped the authority and organized a municipality which they called the Western Provincial Assembly.

Whilst the whites were creating this disturbance of the peace at Saint-Domingue, the National Assembly, uneasy concerning the vengeance of the blacks which would most likely follow the inhuman punishment of Ogé and Chavanne, agreed that the time had come for granting some concessions to the "affranchis." Therefore on May 15, 1791, a decree was adopted stating that free-born colored men would henceforth be eligible to the provincial assemblies. This news upon reaching Saint-Domingue at the end of June, 1791, provoked great excitement. The "affranchis," thinking once more that at last they had acquired the rights which they had been claiming with so much perseverance, showed the wildest enthusiasm; but the whites, whose indignation knew no bounds, protested vigorously against this step; they even went so far as to implore the protection of the English. And pretending that the decree of May 15 had not been officially notified to the Governor of the island, they hastened to elect a new Colonial Assembly with power to regulate the political condition of the "affranchis."

The blacks and mulattoes, regarding this action as a challenge, decided to resort to arms. Having gained wisdom from Ogé's misfortune the "affranchis" this time did not trust to chance.

On August 7, 1791, they held a meeting in the church of Mirebalais and appointed a committee of forty members, of which Pierre Pinchinat was elected president. Whilst this political council was striving to obtain from Mr. de Blanchelande the fair application of the decree of May 15, the colored men of Port-au-Prince, secretly assembled on the plantation of Louise Rabuteau, decided on their military organization (August 21). Beauvais was appointed leader of the insurrection; and it was resolved that the uprising should take place on the 26th of August.

There were already symptoms of an alarmingly dangerous nature affecting the domination of the colonists; the slaves who, up to that time, had been seemingly obedient and resigned, began to show signs of their intention of shaking off the yoke. In June and July insurrections took place at Cul-de-Sac, at Vases, and at Mont-Rouis. The whites had recourse to their usual methods: they tried to intimidate the rebels by inflicting horrible punishments on them. Men were quartered alive; and so great a number was hanged that it was sometimes difficult to find enough executioner.

At that time there appeared before the public a man who was to shape the destinies of his race and have a great influence on the future of Saint-Domingue. Toussaint-Bréda, better known under the name of Louverture, acting in connivance with the followers of the Governor of the island, prepared a general uprising of the slaves. Clever and perspicacious, he assumed at the outset a very modest part. He did not endeavor to obtain the command; his friend Jean-François was proclaimed the leader; Biassou was next in command; to Boukmann and Jeannot had been intrusted the mission of giving the signal of rebellion. This matter settled, there remained but to find a way of influencing all the slaves. These were told that the King of France and the National Assembly had granted them three holidays a week and had abolished flogging as a means of punishment; but that the colonists refused to obey the decree. The slaves, however, after their many years of submission, were naturally cautious; they were afraid of being defeated. Boukmann boldly informed them that soldiers were coming from France to second their revendications. And in order to give them full confidence in themselves he performed an imposing ceremony at "bois Caiman" on August 14, on the plantation of Lenormand de Mézy. On their knees, Boukmann and the conspirators, in the presence of a priestess, took solemn oaths on the reeking entrails of a wild-boar,

Boukmann swearing that he would lead the rebellion, and the others to follow and obey their chief.

Eight days after this "oath of blood," on the night of October 22, the slaves of the Turpin plantation, headed by Boukmann, rose to a man and gave the signal of the struggle for liberty. The slaves of the neighboring plantations hastened to respond to the call of their comrades. The grievances which bad been accumulating for centuries found vent at last. In their turn the masters would be made to suffer the tortures which they had long taken pleasure in inflicting on the unfortunate blacks. In their first paroxysm of anger and revenge the rebels spared neither persons nor things. Armed with pikes, axes, knives, spears,—torch in hand,— they destroyed and exterminated everything that came in their way. Fire and death marked their passage. Jeannot, self-appointed avenger of Ogé and Chavanne, was merciless. In less than eight days 200 sugar refineries and 600 coffee plantations were reduced to ashes; the plain of the North was one immense cemetery.

Jean-François, who had assumed the title of generalissimo and grand-admiral of France, led his followers to the very entrance of Cap-François. On November 14, however, they were defeated; Boukmann was made prisoner and beheaded; his body was then burnt and his head, stuck on the end of a pole, was exposed in the centre of the Place d'Armes of Cap-Français, with a sign bearing the words: "Head of Boukmann, chief of the rebels." The colonists gave no quarter. All the prisoners were at once put to death. Two wheels on which they were tied and their bones broken, and five gallows were kept constantly busy.

Whilst these events were taking place in the North, on August 26, at the Diègue plantation, the "affranchis," in pursuance of the plan adopted on the Rabuteau plantation, took up arms and declared themselves in revolt, with Beauvais at their head. The first encounter took place at the Néret plantation. The whites were defeated; they fled in disorder. From Port-au-Prince troops and artillery were then despatched. A bloody battle was fought on the Pernier plantation. The whites were again defeated, and fled, abandoning their guns, which fell into the hands of the "affranchis." Beauvais then marched with his army to Trou-Caiman, which was fortified.

These two defeats made it clear to the whites that on the battlefield at least the blacks and mulattoes were not their inferiors. Genuinely alarmed by the simultaneous uprising of the slaves and the "affranchis," the wealthy planters thought that the time had come to sever their relations with

France. They sought England's protection and sent to Jamaica for help. The English did not deem that things were ripe for action; in consequence they refused to intervene. Left to themselves, the wealthy planters of Port-au-Prince, in fear of the devastation which had befallen the plain of the North, made up their minds to come to an agreement with the colored men. On October 23, a treaty of peace was signed at the Damiens plantation. By this concordat it was agreed that the "affranchis" would be admitted, on a footing of perfect equality with the whites, in all the assemblies, even in the Colonial Assembly; the sentence against Ogé and his companions would be held in execration and the memory of these martyrs rehabilitated; a solemn mass would be celebrated in all the churches of the Western "département" for these victims, and proper indemnity paid to their widows and children.

When, in pursuance of the treaty of Damiens, the army of colored men entered Port-au-Prince on October 24, Beauvais, its general, and Caradeux, the most aggressive of the planters of Saint-Domingue and commander-in-chief of the militia of the Western "département," were to be seen marching along arm in arm.

In the Artibonite the whites had also signed, on September 22, a concordat with the colored men of

Saint-Marc who had taken up arms under the leadership of Savary.

Everywhere the blacks and mulattoes were victorious. They believed that they had at last acquired their political rights.

Whilst the "affranchis" were deluding themselves with the brightest hopes, their enemies in France did not remain inactive. Their intrigues were carried on with such success that on September 24, 1791, the Constituent Assembly adopted a decree stating that "all laws concerning the position of persons without their freedom, and the state of free colored men and blacks, as well as the regulations for the execution of such laws, would be passed by the now existing and the future Colonial Assemblies. … "

This untimely decree put an end to all the advantages which the "affranchis" had just secured by main force. Henceforth their fate depended on the Colonial Assembly, which was in session at Cap-Français since August 9; on that very assembly whose arrogance and hostility toward the black race were well-known facts.

As soon as the colonists of Port-au-Prince became aware of this decree they did not fail to find a pretext for refusing to ratify the treaty of Damiens. On the morning of November 21 a black man by the name of Scapin, a drummer in

Beauvais's army, had a quarrel with a white soldier; for this he was flogged and afterward hanged by the whites. Valmé, a colored lieutenant, lost no time in avenging Scapin's death by killing a white artilleryman. This was sufficient cause to rekindle the strife. Both sides took up arms again. After a bloody fight, Beauvais, at the head of his army, marched to La Croix-des-Bouquets. Port-au-Prince was on fire. The whites availed themselves of the opportunity afforded by the disorder and confusion which ensued, to massacre all the "affranchis" of whatever age or sex which they met on their way. More than 2,000 mulattresses were put to death. A white man called Larousse killed Madame Beaulieu, a colored woman who was in an advanced state of pregnancy; he opened her abdomen, tore out the child, and threw it into the fire.

The blacks and mulattoes were in a great state of indignation over these atrocities. Their one desire was for vengeance. André Rigaud, who had left for the South, was as not long in returning at the head of a strong army, which he marched as far as Martissant, where he encamped. On the other side, Beauvais besieged Port-au-Prince on the north and on the east. The water supply was cut off. The whole southern portion of the island was in arms.

At Trou Coffin in the neighborhood of Léogane, a Spanish mulatto known as "Romaine-la-Prophétesse" had gathered a large band of followers. He pretended that he had had frequent apparitions of the Blessed Virgin, and in this way he acquired a great amount of influence over his companions.

In the North the slaves were still in arms, their overtures for peace having been contemptuously rejected by the whites.

Such was the situation of the colony when, on November 28, 1791, the first Civil Commissioners, Mirbeck, Roume, and Saint-Léger, arrived at Cap-Français. They had been instructed to restore peace in Saint-Domingue and to enforce the enactment of the Decree of September 24. They tried in vain to restore peace in the island. The arrogant Colonial Assembly of Cap-Français, to which the Decree of September 24 had given special powers, thwarted all their good intentions. The "affranchis" knew only too well the futility of expecting any concessions on the part of the planters; they decided to support the Civil Commissioners, hoping that their assistance would secure for them the recognition of their political rights. On the arrival of Saint-Léger at Port-au-Prince (January, 1792), the leaders of the colored army which was besieging the town immediately requested an interview with him. They showed the greatest deference to the agent of the metropolis. Complying with his request they allowed the city to be revictualed. And in order to entirely win him over, they agreed even to raise the siege: they accordingly returned to La Croix-des-Bouquets.

The whites of Port-au-Prince, highly displeased with Saint-Léger on account of his good disposition toward the colored men, refused to assist him in the repression of the crimes which the followers of "Roumaine-la-Prophétesse" were committing in the plain of Léogane. The "affranchis'" very cleverly profited by this opportunity to make themselves useful: Beauvais and Pinchinat placed a body of 100 soldiers at the disposal of the Civil Commissioner.

Whilst Saint-Léger was at Léogane endeavoring to restore harmony and concord between the colored men and the whites, the planters of Port-au-Prince tried to surprise the army of the "affranchis" quartered at La Croix-des-Bouquets. Being warned in time of the approach of the troops despatched against them, Beauvais and his companions retreated into the mountains of *Grand-Bois and Pensez-y-Bien*. Incensed by the perfidy of the whites, the "affranchis," who up to that time had been very moderate, resorted to radical measures: they roused the slaves of the Cul-de-Sac plain to rebellion. Headed by Hyacinthe, an intelligent and gallant black, these slaves attacked the colonists at La-Croix-des-Bouquets, defeated them and pursued them as far as the neighborhood of Port-au-Prince, which was again besieged (April, 1792).

In the South the struggle still continued between the "affranchis" and the whites; the latter, in order to rid themselves of their foes, called upon their slaves to arm themselves in order to render them assistance.

In the North the slaves who had broken into rebellion tried in vain to make peace. Toussaint, who was not yet known by the name of Louverture, had given the first proof of his perspicacity. Sent to Cap-Français under a flag of truce he was not long in finding out that the Civil Commissioners possessed in reality no power, and that the Colonial Assembly was the supreme authority. Through his advice all parleys were put an end to.

Exposed to the anger of the wealthy planters, hindered by their limited powers and foreseeing grave dangers for the colony, the Civil Commissioners decided to return to France. On April 1, 1792, Mirbeck left Cap-Français; on the 3rd of the same month Saint-Léger sailed from Saint-Marc. Roume, however, remained in Saint-Domingue.

Whilst the foregoing events were taking place in the island of Saint-Domingue, the Constituent Assembly in France had been replaced by the Legislative Assembly. The liberal and generous ideas of the "Girondins" were destined to have a decided influence on the future of the "affranchis." The latter won their first victory at the beginning of December. A decree adopted on the 7th of the same month forbade the use, against the colored men, of the soldiers sent out to the colony. Shortly after this the Legislative Assembly granted to the "affranchis" the equality of political rights for the possession of which so much blood had been shed in Saint Domingue. On March 28, 1792, a decree, approved by the King on April 4, was enacted stating that henceforth free blacks and mulattoes were to have the same political rights as the white colonists; and that, in consequence, they were entitled to participate in the election of the assemblies, to which they were also eligible. Another decree, passed on the 15th and approved on the 22d of June, vested special powers in the Civil Commissioners: instead of being dependent on the Colonial Assembly they were authorized to dissolve that body as well as the other assemblies which were made use of by the colonists so as to undermine the authority of the agents of the mother country.

The Decree of March 28 (better known as the Decree of April 4) was received at Saint-Domingue on May 28. Roume, whose powers had been greatly increased, hastened to have it enrolled by the Colonial Assembly of Cap-Français. With the cooperation of Governor de Blanchelande he decided to subdue the colonists of Port-au-Prince. The "affranchis" gladly tendered their assistance. The colored men of Saint-Marc escorted the Civil Commissioner to La Croix-des-Bouquets (June 20). Soon after Beauvais and Rigaud reoccupied Port-au-Prince (July, 5). The slaves of La Croix-des-Bouquets, l'Arcahaye, and the Cul-de-Sac plain resumed their work. Freedom, however, was granted to 144 of them upon their agreeing to serve for five years in the gendarmery and to help in maintaining order on the plantations.

Whilst Roume was doing his utmost to restore peace at Port-au-Prince, Governor de Blanchelande had gone to Jérémie, accompanied by André Rigaud. The whites of La Grand 'Anse had flatly refused to accept the Decree of April 4. After defeating the colored men, many of the prisoners taken were put to death; the rest were kept in chains on prison-ships in the harbor of Jérémie; among these were even old men, women, and children. The most that Blanchelande could obtain for them was that they be sent to Cap-Français. Satisfied with this relative success he left for Aux Cayes, where he failed in his campaign against the rebellious slaves intrenched at Platons. Disheartened by his defeat he went back to Cap-Français. André Rigaud succeeded in pacifying the rebellious slaves by freeing 700 of them.

Success had at last crowned the efforts of the "affranchis"; by force of arms, blacks and mulattoes had acquired the exercise of their political rights. In the West and in the South more than 1,000 slaves had obtained their freedom. The first blow had been struck at the colonial system!

VI

The Revolution

Sonthonax, Polvérel, and Ailaud, the new Civil Commissioners appointed by France, arrived at Cap-Français on September 18, 1792. They were accompanied by 6,000 soldiers and by General d'Esparbès, the new Governor-General of the island.

The "affranchis," who had already gathered imposing forces, were well prepared to protect and defend by force of arms the rights granted to them by the Decree of April 4, 1792. Their cause was henceforth inseparable from that of the French Revolution. Their assistance was therefore pledged beforehand to the new agents of the mother country.

The condition of the island at this time was not reassuring. In the North the colonists were inflicting punishments of the severest kind on the slaves taken prisoners, without succeeding in quelling the rebellion. In the West and in the South the whites and the "affranchis" were carefully watching each other: symptoms of unrest were rampant. Owing to the want of security resulting, agriculture was neglected and many colonists had left the country.

The Civil Commissioners had hardly become settled when news of the momentous events of August 10 reached Saint-Domingue. The arrest and deposing of Louis XVI furnished the colonists with a pretext for renewing the struggle. The Colonial Assembly tried to stir up the people with a view of getting rid of Sonthonax, Polvérel, and Ailaud. These latter frustrated the plan by taking energetic steps: by an order on October 12 they dissolved the Assembly of Cap-Français and all the other popular assemblies.

In place of the Colonial Assembly they organized what was called the "Commission intermédiaire"(Intermediary Committee), consisting of twelve members: six whites and six colored men. Thus for the first time the representatives of the black race sat, in a political body, by the side of the arrogant colonists who formerly had had naught but contempt for them. Pinchinat, Jacques Borno, Louis Boisrond, François Raymond, Castaing, and Latortue were the first "affranchis" officially admitted to the honor of participating in the administration of the colony. The colored men did not content themselves with belonging simply to the Intermediary Committee, they took a large part in the organization of the municipalities; they even held public offices. Civil and political equality was henceforth an accomplished fact. But much blood was still to be shed; and the black race was to struggle heroically and successfully to preserve forever an advantage for the winning of which so many lives had been sacrificed.

The pride of the colonists suffered greatly; it seemed impossible for them to accept such a situation. At Cap-Français they plotted a conspiracy, in which even the new Governor-General, d'Esparbès, took part. The Civil Commissioners were able to prevent disturbances only by resorting to extraordinary measures. Assured of the devotedness of the colored men, they proceeded without hesitation to arrest General d'Esparbès and forty white officers, all of whom were taken on board and kept as prisoners in the harbor of Cap-Français. General Rochambeau became acting Governor-General. For a while the firm attitude of the Civil Commissioners preserved peace. They thought that they could now safely look after the welfare of the various provinces. Polvérel left for the West and Ailaud for the South. Sonthonax remained at Cap-Français with the Intermediary Committee. Instead of going to Aux Caves, Ailaud, alarmed by the existing state of things, abandoned his post and returned to France. Sonthonax therefore went South in his place. In January, 1793, he had barely finished expelling from Platons the rebellious slaves of the plain of Cayes, when grave events compelled him to leave the South. Fighting had already taken place in the streets of Cap-Français (December 2, 1792): a body of white soldiers had refused to acknowledge the authority of a colored officer appointed to command them; they mutinied. A few colonists and the sailors of the men-of-war hastened to side with the white soldiers. They attacked the battalion of colored men, who, after a fierce defense, were compelled to yield to the superior forces of their opponents; they withdrew to Haut-du-Cap, where they took possession of the artillery. On his arrival at Cap-Français, Sonthonax arrested and embarked the most important factionists. The colored soldiers agreed then to return to Cap-Français; they were welcomed with great honor: the Civil Commissioner, the acting Governor, the Intermediary Committee, and the municipality all went to meet them. This reception irritated the colonists of Cap-Français, and more especially those of Port-au-Prince. The latter, in order to avenge what they considered as a humiliation put upon the white race, plotted the expulsion of the Civil Commissioners and the extermination of the colored men when the agents of France would be no longer in the island to protect them.

For a while they forgot their own differences and united firmly against their common enemy. In their turn they succeeded in stirring up against the colored men the slaves of "Fond-Parisien" and of the Cul-de-Sac plain. The revolt broke out on January 23, 1793. Thirty-three plantations belonging to colored men were reduced to ashes. Emboldened by their success the wealthy planters of Port-au-Prince, headed by Auguste Borel, arrested General Lasalle, then acting Governor. Rochambeau bad been sent to Martinique. General Lasalle succeeded in making his escape; he went to Saint-Marc, where Sonthonax had already arrived; Polvérel soon joined them. The colored men hastened to render to the Civil Commissioners all the assistance in their power. A strong army marched against Port-au-Prince. After a hard and desperate straggle the town surrendered. Beauvais was appointed commander-in-chief of the militia of the West; and a body of regular troops, "the Legion of Equality," was organized, with the mulatto Antoine Chanlatte as its colonel.

Their authority once more established in Port-au-Prince, Polvérel and Sonthonax tried to subdue La Grand'Anse. For this purpose they despatched a delegation accompanied by 1200 soldiers under the command of André Rigaud. The colonists of that portion of Saint-Domingue had gradually rid themselves of the control of the agents appointed by France; they had elected an Administrative Council at Jérémie, which voted even taxes. They had armed their slaves and placed at their head a black man by the name of Jean Kina. Aided by them they had succeeded in expelling from their "département" all the "affranchis," blacks and mulattoes. The army of the colonists was intrenched at Desrivaux. André Rigaud attacked it on June 19, 1793. He was completely defeated. After their victory the whites of La Grand'Anse transformed their Administrative Council into a Council of Safety and Execution (Conseil de Sûreté et d'Exécution), which they vested with extraordinary powers.

In the mean time, the greatest excitement was prevailing once more at Cap-Français. The Governor of the island, General Galbaud, had espoused the interests of the colonists. Upon the arrival of Polvérel and Sonthonax in that town, all the inhabitants were plotting against them. But having with them a battalion of colored men with Antoine Chanlatte in command, they felt that they were sufficiently powerful to order Galbaud to immediately leave the island and sail for France (June 13). The Governor raised a rebellion among the crew of the men-of-war; and on June 20 he landed at Cap-Français at the head of 3,000 men. Antoine Chanlatte, gallantly supported by Jean-Baptiste Belley, a free black, lost no time in going to the help of the Commissioners. A bloody struggle occurred in the streets of Cap-Français. In the end, however, Polvérel and Sonthonax were compelled to abandon the town, which was left to the mercy of Galbaud's sailors. On the 21st of June they retreated to Camp-Bréda. Their situation seemed hopeless. That very day they issued a decree promising full freedom to all the slaves who would take up arms for the cause of the French Republic, promising also that they would be considered the equals of the whites and would enjoy all the rights belonging to the French citizens. As soon as this decree became known to them, the followers of Pierrot, Macaya, and Goa, who were fighting on their own behalf, hastened to place themselves at the disposal of the representatives of the French Republic. With a firm determination to earn their freedom, these slaves fiercely attacked the forces of Galbaud; owing to their assistance Cap-Français was stormed on June 23. The sailors had sacked and partly destroyed the unfortunate town by fire. The ill-fated island of Saint-Domingue continued thus to be devastated by fire and sword.

Instead of improving, the situation of the Civil Commissioners daily grew worse. In February France was again at war with Great Britain; hostilities soon followed with Spain. The representatives of France and Spain at Saint-Domingue were both instructed by their respective governments to spare no pains, to resort even to the revolted slaves, in order to conquer the territory of the other party. The Governor of the Spanish portion of the island was already carrying out these instructions. He had won over Jean-Francois, Biassou, and Toussaint Louverture, whom he loaded with favors and honors. Jean-François was appointed lieutenant-general of the forces of the King of Spain; Toussaint Louverture became major-general (maréchal-de-camp). "For the first time black slaves were to be seen bedecked with ribbons, crosses and other insignia of nobility."

Encouraged by the rewards granted to them, pleased with the equality of treatment existing between the white Spaniards and themselves, the blacks fought valiantly. By their victories the French portion of Saint-Domingue was in jeopardy. After Galbaud's defeat, many of the white officers, indignant at the ever-increasing influence of the colored men, had begun to betray the cause of France. One after the other, Ouanaminthe, the important camp of La Tannerie, and the Lesec camp were turned over to the Spaniards. The victorious followers of Jean-Francois, Baissou, and Toussaint Louverture had taken possession of almost the whole northern province.

In the South, the colonists of the "Grand'Anse," availing themselves of the defeat of André Rigaud, had again sought the protection of the English. As soon as peace with France was at an end, the representatives of these proud and haughty planters had hastened to submit to the English Government plans for the occupation of Saint-Domingue (February 25, 1793). On September 3, 1793, Venault de Charmilly, acting on behalf of the colonists, and Adam Williamson, representing Great Britain, signed at St. Iago de la Vega the agreement which was destined to put the country into the hands of France's enemies. And on September 19 the English soldiers, under the command of Lieutenant-Colonel Whitelocke, landed at Jérémie; cries of "Long live King George!" "Long live the English!" were heard on all sides. There were thus Frenchmen who, blinded by their hatred of the colored men, preferred to betray their country and to give up to its foes a portion of its territory, rather than submit to the necessity of admitting equality of political rights granted to the free blacks and mulattoes.

On September 22 the English, without striking a blow, occupied also Môle Saint-Nicolas. They were soon in possession of L'Arcahaie, Leogane, Saint-Marc, and of the whole province of La Grand'Anse.

It looked as if France was about to lose possession of Saint-Domingue. In the North the only important places where the French authority was still acknowledged were Fort-Dauphin, Cap-Français, and Port-de-Paix, where General Laveaux, the acting Governor, resided. Yet the Civil Commissioners had not remained inactive whilst these events were taking place. In June they had tried without success to alienate Jean-François, Biassou, and Toussaint Louverture from the Spanish cause. In July Polvérel left for the West, where hostile manifestations against France were threatened. Won over by the Spaniards, two brothers named Guyambois, blacks who had gained their freedom, were planning, first to place three chiefs at the head of the colony—Jean Guyambois, Jean-Francois, and Biassou; secondly, to proclaim the freedom of all the slaves; and third, to share the land among the former slaves. A Frenchman, the Marquis d'Espinville, in connivance with the Spanish Governor, encouraged these schemes. Polvérel frustrated the plot by arresting the two Guyambois and the principal accomplices. However, great excitement prevailed among the slaves when news of this project became known. It was feared that they would be completely won over to the Spanish cause through the promise of freedom and of the partition of the land. Thus the concession made by the Decree of June 21, which granted freedom alone to those slaves who would fight for the French Republic, lost a great deal of its importance. Therefore it became necessary to take more liberal measures. On August 21 Polvérel ordered that all persons found guilty of specified crimes would forfeit their movable and landed property. And on August 27 he issued a decree stating first that the Africans or their descendants who would remain on or return to the plantations considered vacant would become free and would enjoy all the rights exercised by the French citizens, provided they agreed to work on the said plantations; secondly, that all the vacant plantations of the West would belong in common to those inhabitants of the province who had borne arms for the French and to the cultivators of those plantations; thirdly, that (first) all the rebellious blacks who would reinstate or help to reinstate the Republic in the possession of the territory occupied by its enemies, all those who would swear allegiance to the Republic and fight for it, (secondly) all the Spaniards, all the revolted Africans, either maroons or independent, who would facilitate the conquest of the Spanish portion of the island—all these would benefit by the partition that would be made of the vacant plantations; and, fourthly, that all real estate belonging to the Spanish Government, to the nobles, to the friars and priests would be distributed among the warriors and cultivators.

Polvérel boldly asserted the principle of the dispossession of the colonists in behalf of the slaves; yet he abstained from saying the words so eagerly desired by them—general freedom. However, circumstances had made such a step unavoidable. In the North important events were occurring daily. On August 25 a white man, Gr. H. Vergniaud, seneschal at Cap-Français, had presented a petition to Sonthonax in which the full measure of justice was requested. The situation was very critical; the assistance of the blacks was indispensable in order to check the progress of the Spaniards. Sonthonax hesitated no longer; he proclaimed general freedom. His decree of August 29 restored at last to human dignity thousands of men who for centuries had bent beneath the shameful yoke of slavery. Article 12 of this decree ordered that a third of the products of every plantation be divided among the cultivators.

Surprised by the radical measures taken by Sonthonax, Polvérel was at first uncertain as to what course he should pursue. But the impatience of the slaves, the growing dangers which threatened the colony, soon decided him to adopt his colleague's views.

Thinking that an imposing ceremony should accompany such a step he ordered a general gathering at the Place d'Armes in Port-au-Prince of all the citizens, white and colored; and on September 21, 1793, the anniversary of the establishment of the French Republic, he publicly declared, at the "autel de la Patrie," that slavery was abolished in all the communes of the West. In their enthusiasm many slave-owners signed their adherence to this great act of social reparation, on registers previously prepared for that purpose. Two days after, the name of Port-au-Prince was changed to Port-Républicain, "in order that the inhabitants be kept continually in mind of the obligations which the French revolution imposed on them."

On October 6, 1793, Polvérel, then at Cayes, freed the slaves of the South. Thus the coalition of the wealthy planters of Saint-Domingue with the English and the Spaniards had the effect of hastening the abolition of the very institution of slavery which it was their intention to preserve and maintain in the colony had their efforts been crowned with success.

After two long years of struggle and of suffering the blacks eventually were delivered forever from this barbarous and inhuman system. In Saint-Domingue men would no longer be the property of men. The revolution was complete. It remained but for the logic of events to accomplish the rest.

In the mean time, the Civil Commissioners were bestowing the highest offices on colored men, the white officers having proved untrustworthy; after the execution of Louis XVI they had not scrupled to give up their forces to the Spaniards. In Polvérel's absence, Pinchinat was invested with all the civil powers in the West. Montbrun was Commander-in-chief of the province; Antoine Chanlatte had the military posts under his authority; Beauvais was in command at Mirebalais and La Croix-des-Bouquets; Greffin at Léogane; Brunache at Petit-Goave; Faubert at Baynet; Doyon at L 'Anse-à-

Veau, etc. André Rigaud was commander-in-chief of the South. At the end of 1793 the taking of possession of power by the colored men was an accomplished fact. And they were about to justify the trust which France had placed in them by bravely defending her territory against foreign invaders.

*

At the beginning of 1794 the English were in possession of Arcahaie, Léogane, Môle-Saint-Nicolas, Jérémie, and of the whole province of La Grand'Anse. In the North the Spaniards occupied Gros-Morne, Plaisance, Lacul, Limbé, Port-Margot, Borgne, Terre-Neuve, etc. On December 6, 1793, Toussaint Louverture, who was fighting for Spain, became master of Gonaives. General Laveaux, appointed acting Governor-General by Sonthonax, was at Port-de-Paix; and the mulatto Villate held the highest military command at Cap-Français. On leaving the latter place for Port-au-Prince, the Civil Commissioner transferred his powers to the mulatto Péré. Thus a Governor-General, a military commander and a civil delegate were all three in command at a time when circumstances called for unity of action.

Sonthonax left Cap-Français in a state of great indignation at the defections which were daily increasing the number of France's enemies. The wealthy planters and the European officers espoused the Spanish cause—they did not scruple even to join the followers of Jean-François, Biassou, and Toussaint Louverture. The very men who a few years previous had had naught but the utmost contempt for the slaves were now helping these very slaves to wage war on their own country. Some colored men such as Savary, at Saint-Marc, and Jean-Baptiste Lapointe at L'Arcahaie, following the example given them by the whites, in their turn betrayed the trust placed in them. Their conduct angered Sonthonax to such a degree that he began to distrust indiscriminately all the colored men. Then began the unfortunate policy of division which was destined to bring about disastrous consequences, the bad effects of which it has been so difficult to root out in Haiti.

In July, 1793, Polvérel and Sonthonax had written to the mulattoes, trying to incite them against the whites and cautioning them to be on their guard concerning the general freedom of the slaves. However, it so happened that events had made this dreaded general freedom an accomplished fact. Therefore those desirous of exploiting either the mulattoes or the blacks had to resort to the *divide et impera* maxim. In consequence nothing was spared to excite the mutual jealousy of the men of the black race and to sow discord among them.

In the mean time, Sonthonax, on his arrival at Port-au-Prince, had ordered the disbanding of the militia. He set free Guyambois, who had been imprisoned by Polvérel for having been the leader in the conspiracy which was destined to place Saint-Domingue under the authority of a triumvirate consisting of himself, Jean-François, and Biassou. Through Guyambois, Sonthonax entered into relations with Halaou, a black chief, who, in order to preserve his influence over his followers, pretended to be in communication with Heaven through a white cock which was his inseparable companion. The Civil Commissioner invited Halaou to Port-au-Prince, where a banquet was given in his honor at the Executive Mansion. A report that the death of Beauvais, who was at La Croix-des-Bouquets, was decided upon, began to be noised abroad. Upon leaving Port-au-Prince the black leader unfortunately went to La Croix-des-Bouquets; this step served to confirm the rumor which had been set afloat. In consequence, Pinchinat and Montbrun made up their minds to do away with him; and Marc Borno undertook to carry out the criminal project. He started at once for La

Croix-des-Bouquets, where, on his arrival, he ordered a sergeant to kill Halaou. A bloody fight ensued, in which the followers the latter were defeated. This murder was provoked by the instigation wrongly or rightly attributed to Sonthonax, who did nothing to conceal his distrust of the colored men. He soon appointed as commandant of "the place" of Port-au-Prince the white General Desfourneaux, who, having been arrested by Polvérel's order, and tried by a court martial presided over by Montbrun, harbored a bitter grudge against this mulatto officer. Montbrun was the highest military authority at Port-au-Prince. The appointment of this new officer was not to his liking. His displeasure increased, when, contrary to hierarchic discipline, Desfourneaux was directly authorized by Sonthonax to supply a regiment with new soldiers. The commandant of the place availed himself of the opportunity to enlist and arm all the whites, whose hostility toward the colored men was a recognized fact. The latter, blacks and mulattoes, who formed the "Legion of Equality" under the command of Montbrun, became uneasy. A conflict was thus made inevitable; it occurred during the night of March 17, 1794. Montbrun's soldiers attacked and defeated Desfourneaux's. The streets of Port-au-Prince were again stained with blood at a time when the union of all its inhabitants was of absolute necessity to its successful defense.

At the beginning of January, 1794, an English squadron, under the command of Commodore John Ford, had appeared in the harbor. The energetic refusal of Sonthonax to surrender the city had impressed the English; they withdrew without making any attack. But they were not long in returning with stronger forces. On May 30 their fleet was again in the harbor. The landing forces, with General White at their head, were reinforced by the French counter-revolutionists under the command of Baron de Montalembert, H. de Jumécourt, and Lapointe. Against this army of about 3,000 men Port-au-Prince could not oppose more than 1,100 soldiers. The English occupied the city on June 4. Thereupon the Civil Commissioners retreated to Jacmel, when on June 8 the corvette *L'Espérance* arrived from France. Captain Chambon notified them of the decree of impeachment adopted against them by the Convention on July 16, 1793. The Commissioners lost no time in sailing, leaving the defense of the colony to the care of Laveaux in the North and of Rigaud in the South.

Before leaving Jacmel, Polvérel wrote to Rigaud on June 11, denouncing Montbrun as a traitor. Yet the Civil Commissioners took no steps to have the traitor court-martialed; instead of this he continued to exercise his powers as Governor of the West. Thus to the mulatto Rigaud fell the task of arresting and dismissing the mulatto Montbrun, which served but to foster distrust and jealousy.

After the departure of the Civil Commissioners two military chiefs were in command in the colony: Laveaux and Rigaud. A great portion of the territory was occupied by the English and the Spaniards.

At this period the outlook was a gloomy one for France, which seemed rapidly to be losing hold of her colony. At this juncture a man destined to be the most celebrated representative of the black race turned the scales by the weight of his influence and of his sword: Toussaint Louverture deserted the Spanish cause and took up that of France. The prestige of his name sufficed to expel the Spaniards from Gonaives Marmelade, Plaisance, Gros-Morne, d'Ennery, Dondon, and Limbé. The famous name of this great man should not be passed over without a few words as to his life and character. Born on the Bréda plantation at Haut du Cap, Toussaint spent the first fifty years of his life in slavery; "and," says Placide Justin, "this humble condition did not prevent him from reaching the pinnacle of military honors and from rising, not only above the men of his own race, but above the haughty whites, who were compelled to acknowledge his superiority and wisdom." He began life as a herdsman, during which period he occupied his leisure hours in learning to read and write, and in studying the medicinal plants of the country. He afterward became coachman of Bayou de Libertat, then the manager of the Bréda plantation. Toussaint soon won the confidence of his master. Through his knowledge he already had great influence over the men of his race. It was owing to this that he was so instrumental in bringing about the uprising of the slaves in 1791. But he was wise enough not to assume at the outset a prominent part. In this manner he could not be charged with the responsibility of any of the numerous incendiary fires and murders which accompanied the first great manifestation of the slaves; on the contrary he protected Mr. de Libertat and his family, and exerted all the means in his power to find a safe shelter for them until he could facilitate their departure from Saint-Domingue. When success loomed in the future, Toussaint joined the followers of Biassou, whose secretary he became; he had assumed the title of "Doctor of the King's Armies." This title he changed, however, in June, 1793, and styled himself "General of the King's Army." He followed Jean-François and Biassou when they espoused the Spanish cause. But they became jealous of his success at the head of the army he had organized; and Biassou affected to treat his former secretary as if he were still his subordinate. Relying on his influence over his companions and profiting by the prestige resulting from Ms victories over the French, Toussaint threw off the control exercised over him by his former chiefs and declared that he would henceforth receive orders from no one but the representatives of the King of Spain. The conflict became so acute that his soldiers attacked Biassou's. The latter sent a petition to the Governor of the Spanish portion of Saint-Domingue in which the French emigrants who were at Fort Dauphin denounced Toussaint Louverture as a murderer and a traitor; they even requested that he should be put to death. Don Cabrera went so far as to arrest his whole family, including his nephew Moise. The arrest of his relatives showed Toussaint that, in spite of the great services he had rendered them, the Spaniards were inclined to believe that the charges brought against him were not without foundation. At any moment he might be dismissed, imprisoned, and put to death. These considerations perhaps largely influenced him in deciding to join the cause of France; but they were assuredly not the only reasons which determined his decision; the general freedom granted to the slaves, the political rights which blacks and mulattoes enjoyed under the French and which were still denied them by the Spaniards, had also their effect in influencing him. Be it as it may, on the 4th of May, 1794, the French flag was again hoisted at Gonaives: Toussaint Louverture had abandoned the Spaniards. This defection was in itself a revolution. It was destined to settle the fate of a whole race. However, it was France that for the time being was to profit by it.

Unsuccessful in his attack against Saint Marc where Major Brisbane was in command, Toussaint Louverture made up for his defeat by taking possession of Les Verettes, le Pont de l'Ester, and La Petite-Rivière; he expelled the Spaniards from Saint Raphael, Saint Michel, Hinche, and Dondon.

Whilst Toussaint was reconquering for France the portion of her territory formerly occupied by her enemies, Andre Rigaud, on the night of October 5, 1794, attacked and entered Léogane; he also occupied "Fort Ça-Ira" and "l'Acul" in spite of the energetic resistance made by the English. On December 29 the latter, under command of Lieutenant-Colonel Bradford, were again defeated by Rigaud in his attack on Tiburon. Cast down by this blow, Bradford committed suicide.

Beauvais also had been active in expelling from Saltrou the English and the French emigrants who were threatening Jacmel. Owing to Laveaux, whose firmness of attitude at Port-de-Paix had checked the English, to Villate who defended Cap-Français against the attacks by land and sea of the combined forces of the Spaniards and the English, to Toussaint Louverture who reconquered almost the whole Northern province, to Rigaud who retook Léogane and kept nearly the whole Southern province under his authority, the year 1794 which had dawned so disastrously for France drew to a close with the foreign invaders having but a gloomy outlook before them.

Therefore the English, who seemed to believe that all means were fair in war, did not hesitate to resort to corruption. They attempted to win over Rigaud to them by offering him a bribe of 3,000,000 francs. The colored officer rejected with scorn this shameful proposal. A similar attempt at bribery was made on Laveaux, to whom only 50,000 francs were offered. Did the English consider the honor of a white less valuable than that of a colored man? The Governor of Saint-Domingue resented the affront; in his indignation he challenged Colonel Whitelock, who had made the proposal to a duel, to which the latter paid no heed. The English were guilty of a still graver offense. Having captured seventy soldiers of the Southern Legion, they sent them to Jamaica, where, by order of Adam Williamson, Governor of the

Island, the captives were imprisoned, chained by the neck; and in spite of the fact that they were prisoners of war, they were publicly sold as slaves. Yet Rigaud and his officers were kind in their treatment of 400 sailors of the *Switchoold* that had been captured at Cayes.

Following the advice of the French colonists, the English restored slavery and established the supremacy of the whites throughout the territory they occupied. Nevertheless, they had among their followers mulattoes and black leaders like Jean Kina and Hyacinthe. Being thus warned of the fate in store for them, should the English be successful, and tranquilized by the Decree of February 4, 1794, by which the National Convention confirmed the general freedom granted by Sonthonax and Polvérel and abolished slavery in all the French colonies, the colored men began to plot on behalf of France. Their conspiracy was discovered at Saint Marc and L'Arcahaie, and they were mercilessly put to death. Elsewhere, however, their defection favored Toussaint's designs.

In February, 1795, Major Brisbane, who was in command at Saint-Marc, attacked the forces of Toussaint Louverture; the English officer was defeated and severely wounded. In his dealings with the prisoners made by him Toussaint acted with great caution. He would not shoot the French colonists and emigrants, but would send them to Laveaux, who had to take the responsibility of putting them to death. In this way he began to befriend the whites.

Throughout all the time that war was being waged, Toussaint never allowed the cultivation of the land to be neglected. With money raised from the products of the soil he was able to buy arms and ammunition from the United States. Rigaud in the South, and Beauvais in the West, also encouraged agriculture; Cayes and Jacmel could in this way entertain an active commercial intercourse with the United States.

The officers to whose care was intrusted the defense of Saint-Domingue had only their own resources upon which to rely. France was in so critical a condition that there was no probability of her sending any help to the colony, which was even without any news from the mother country. The English, on the other hand, received reinforcements in April, 1795. Considerably strengthened by the assistance of the Spaniards and the arrival of the new soldiers, they extended their authority to Mirebalais, Las Cahobas, and Banica. Before long, however, they were destined to be deprived of the support of their allies. On July 22, 1795, the Treaty of Bale was signed and Spain gave up the whole Spanish portion of Saint-Domingue to France.

At about the same time, on July 23, the National Convention adopted a decree stating that the army of Saint-Domingue had well deserved of the country, and appointing Laveaux major-general and Villate, Toussaint Louverture, Beauvais, and Rigaud brigadier-generals. This good news was brought to Saint-Domingue by the sloop of war *Venus*, which anchored at Cap-Français the 14th of October, 1795. Laveaux, who up to that time had been residing at Port-de-Paix, returned to Cap-Français, which Villate had so valiantly defended against the English and the Spaniards. Taking advantage of the Treaty of Bale, the Governor of Saint-Domingue demanded the restitution of the whole portion of the French territory occupied by the Spaniards; he insisted upon having Jean-François sent out of the country. On January 4, 1796, the black leader left Fort Dauphin for Havana. He died in Spain, where he had kept his rank of lieutenant-general.

The English, however, thought that Jean-François's followers might be useful to them. To win them over to their cause they had recourse to a black man named Titus, whom they supplied with money and arms. Obeying Laveaux's orders Villate attacked and stormed the camp organized by Titus. The latter was killed and his followers dispersed.

In spite of the services rendered to France by Villate, Laveaux never trusted him. From Port-de-Paix, where he resided, he used to watch every movement of the military commander of Cap-Français.

As a matter of fact, Laveaux was displeased at his being kept in the background. As Governor of Saint-Domingue he had now but the native troops to rely on for maintaining his authority; and these he believed more devoted to the officers of their own color than to him. The European officers, the colonists, the royalists, the reactionists had no scruple at going over to the Spaniards and the English. It was not possible to intrust to them the mission of defending the colony. France had thus to resort to the colored men, who constituted the majority of the first freedmen; they rose then to the foremost rank by mere force of circumstances. Through their own fault the whites had lost their preeminence. Rigaud had all the power in the South, Beauvais in the West, and Villate at Cap-Français. The two first fully acknowledged Laveaux's authority; they never failed to keep him aware of their doings. Their devotion to France could not be questioned; they acted bravely in defense of her territory against the English. Villate alone was at variance with the Governor of Saint-Domingue. Nevertheless, the latter deemed it fit to hold all the mulattoes responsible for his quarrel with his subordinate at Cap-Français.

Union Club, Cap Haitien

Laveaux pompously charged them with plotting to make Saint-Domingue an independent State, in order to be alone in command; he took umbrage at their growing influence, of which France, however, was deriving the greatest benefit. Such was the frame of mind he was in when Toussaint Louverture deserted the Spanish cause.

Clever and perspicacious, Toussaint at once saw the way in which to turn the mistrust of Laveaux to his own advantage. The latter became a mere puppet in his hands. Beneath his affected mildness was hidden an energetic will; his ambition knew no bounds. Everything must yield before him. Woe to those who dared to stand in his way. Conscious of his superiority over Laveaux, whose narrow-mindedness he was not long in finding out, he proposed to carry out his own interests, under the pretext of accomplishing the Governor's designs. The Agents of France sought to cripple the power of the mulattoes who had given offense to them, thinking that once deprived of their natural allies the blacks easily could be taken back to the deserted plantations.

Toussaint Louverture's intention was to help to reduce the influence of the mulattoes, but in his own behalf and at the expense of those who thought to use him as a tool which they would afterward throw aside. The black man was to prove more clever and a better tactician than the white. The time for action was nearing.

The inhabitants of Cap-Français, displeased with the administration of the Governor, rebelled on March 20, 1796. Laveaux was arrested and imprisoned. The municipality of Cap-Français hastened to adopt a decree investing Villate with the Governorship. This officer, instead of doing his duty by repressing the riot, accepted the office conferred on him by the municipality; thus becoming an accomplice in the attack made upon his official superior. The black Colonels Léveillé and Pierre-Michel protested against such an action. The latter through the medium of Henri Christophe, then a captain, wrote to the municipality demanding the release of Laveaux. He gathered at Fort Belair the black officers Pierrot, Barthélemy, Flaville, etc. Toussaint Louverture intervened energetically on behalf of the Governor. He threatened to lead an attack on Cap-Français if Laveaux were not immediately set free. Such an attitude decided the municipality to reconsider its action. On March 22 Laveaux was set at liberty and Villate withdrew to La Martellière camp. The Governor, however, did not consider himself in safety at Cap-Français; accordingly he went to Petite-Anse, where soon new riots occurred. On March 28 Toussaint came to his help. Two days later the blacks at Cap-Français took up arms; they had been told that Laveaux intended to reestablish slavery. Toussaint Louverture restored order; he became henceforth indispensable and was master of the situation. Entirely discredited, Laveaux was no longer able to maintain his authority except with the support of his former protégé: he appointed Toussaint

Lieutenant-Governor. Toussaint was turning to his advantage the mistakes and passions of all.

Whilst Villate was committing the fault of participating in the arrest of the representative of France, Rigaud and his followers were valiantly defending the tricolor flag.

Great Britain had sent heavy reinforcements to Saint-Domingue. In command of over 3,000 men, General Bowyer and Admiral Parker left Port-au-Prince on March 20, 1796; on the 21st the combined land and sea forces attacked Léogane. Alexandre Pétion, who was at that time a major in the army, was in command of Fort Ça-Ira; he compelled the English fleet to withdraw. Renaud Desruisseaux successfully repelled the two assaults made upon Léogane. The English hastened to return to Port-au-Prince when they heard that Beauvais, from Jacmel, and Rigaud, from Cayes, were moving with the greatest haste to aid in defending the town.

In the mean time the Directory had been authorized, by an act adopted on January 24, 1796, to send five Agents to Saint-Domingue. Roume, Sonthonax, Juien Raymond, Giraud, and Leblanc were appointed. Roume was to reside at Santo Domingo. Pie arrived there on April 8, 1796; and his four colleagues landed at Cap-Français on May 12. The new Agents were accompanied by Major-

General Rochainbeau, in command of the Spanish portion of the island, Major-General Desfourneaux, and Brigadier-Generals Martial Besse, A. Chanlatte, Beclot, and Lesuire.

The day after their arrival the Agents ordered Villate to appear before them. He therefore returned to Cap-Français, where he was given an enthusiastic welcome by the inhabitants. Displeased with this friendly attitude toward his opponent, Laveaux, at the head of a detachment, charged the crowd: 45 women were wounded.

Villate was at first sent back to his camp; but afterward he was sentenced to be deported and outlawed. To avoid bloodshed he left on the frigate *Méduse* for France, where he was tried and acquitted.

When Sonthonax left for France in 1794 he already bore feelings of enmity against the mulattoes; he came back to Saint-Domingue with the determination to exert every means in his power to destroy their influence. He found it comparatively easy to carry out his plan; for Laveaux had the same design. There was in consequence nothing else to do but to continue the policy already adopted, and the object of which was to use the blacks against the mulattoes in order to restore to the whites the supremacy which they had lost; afterward the blacks would be dealt with.

At the time when the peace of Bale made it possible to undertake an energetic campaign against the English, the agents of France spent their time in sowing and fostering discord everywhere, instead of trying to unite all those who were willing to defend the cause of the mother country.

Soon after appointing Toussaint Louverture major-general they sent a delegation of three members, Rey, Leborgne and Keverseau, to the South for the purpose of controlling the administration of that province; they decided to cause the arrest of Pinchinat, who was universally esteemed and whose influence was feared by Sonthonax. This delegation arrived at Cayes on June 23, 1796, increased by the addition of Desfourneaux in the capacity of General Inspector of the troops of the South and the West. It was this same General Desfourneaux whose intrigues had provoked an armed conflict in Port-au-Prince on March 17, 1794. Having suffered defeat at the hands of the mulatto Monthbrun, he was, like Sonthonax and Laveaux, unfriendly toward the colored men. Another of the delegates, Rey, having been implicated in an attempt to murder Andre Rigaud in 1793, had been compelled to flee from Caves. And this was the man who had been sent there as the official superior of this general. In this manner Sonthonax and his colleagues plainly showed how slightly they minded wounding the feelings of Andre Rigaud, who, however, had been the one to drive away the English from Léogane and Tiburon, who had kept order and discipline in the whole Southern province, and whose devotion to France could not be questioned. Rigaud's crime consisted in the confidence reposed in him by both blacks and mulattoes, and, in consequence, his influence over them. They charged him with striving for the independence of Saint-Domingue and with keeping out the whites from public offices. Yet at Cayes on the arrival of the delegates two white Frenchmen occupied the position of Orderer (ordonnateur) and Controller of the Treasury, and they were so successful in their management of the finances that the Southern province was able to subsist on its own resources. On account of their devotion to Andre Rigaud, however, they were dismissed and replaced by mere tools of the Agents. The squandering of the people's money began. The order for the arrest of Pinchinat increased the discontent of the inhabitants. But he could not be found, for on July 17 he had left Cayes, taking shelter in the Baradères Mountains.

In order to establish their authority more firmly the Delegates were eager to win a few victories over the English. In consequence they instructed Rigaud to storm the fortified place of "Irois" and

Desfourneaux was ordered to attack the Davezac camp. On the 7th of August Rigaud assaulted Irois but failed in his attack; he retreated to Tiburon. On his side Desfourneaux, who was accompanied by the Delegates, was equally unsuccessful in his attempt at storming the Raimond camp; he had to withdraw to the Perrin camp. This double defeat in thwarting the plans of the Delegates so irritated them that they were unable to conceal their disappointment. In their report they said that "they could maintain their authority only by fighting the English. A victory together with the kind treatment they intended to extend to the vanquished were to lead them from the South to the North. The colony would be saved and the Frenchmen would be once more its masters."

The blacks and mulattoes were not then considered as Frenchmen. According to the Delegates the whites alone were capable of being the masters of Saint-Domingue. In case of success their intention therefore was to come to an understanding with the colonists of the Grand'Anse, who were known to entertain the greatest hostility toward the members of the black race. The Agents of France who were at Cap-Français had already issued an amnesty in favor of the emigrants and colonists who would join the French cause.

After their defeat the delegates returned to Cayes (August 18, 1796). They dismissed the "Commandant of the Arrondissement," Augustin Rigaud, the brother of General André Rigaud, and replaced him by Beauvais. Their idea in taking this step was that such an appointment could not fail to create bad feeling between André Rigaud and Beauvais, who were both brigadier-generals; they expected that the latter would show much reluctance in obeying the former's orders: consequently rivalry and conflict, they imagined, would surely ensue between the two mulatto generals. Their forces being thus weakened by division, General Desfourneaux would be justified in putting them aside and in assuming the command of the Southern province. The scheme failed owing to too great haste in bringing about the desired result. The Commandant of Arrondissement of Saint-Louis, the mulatto Lefranc, seeming to stand in their way, the delegates decided to get rid of him. He therefore was ordered to proceed to Cayes where, on his arrival, Desfourneaux caused him to be arrested. Whilst being taken on board *L'Africaine*, he succeeded in making his escape and fled to the Fort La Tourterelle, where he fell in with the soldiers of the regiment which had been formerly under his command. André Rigaud was at that time at Tiburon. In the fight which ensued

Desfourneaux's soldiers were defeated. In the plain of Cayes, on the night of August 28, Augustin Rigaud stirred up an insurrection among the blacks whom the emissaries of the delegates were provoking against the mulattoes. A few whites were murdered. Desfourneaux and Rey, alarmed by the popular movement, hurriedly left Cayes. Leborgne and Keverseau, who remained at their post, sent immediately for André Rigaud, whose assistance Lefranc and Augustin had also sought. On the arrival of the colored general (August 31) special powers were conferred on him by the delegates. For the purpose of restoring order they were obliged to have recourse to the very man whose influence they had sought to annihilate.

Quiet speedily prevailed. And the measures taken by Rigaud were so efficacious that the captains of the American ships in the harbor of Cayes extended their thanks to him for the protection he offered them.

After having adopted and pursued in a still worse degree the policy followed by Laveaux in setting the blacks against the mulattoes, Sonthonax and his colleagues tried to cast upon Toussaint the responsibility of the discord which they had fomented. In their report to the Directory of the events which occurred in Saint-Domingue they wrote the following: "Some of the black generals remained faithful. They rescued General Laveaux by force. Two opposite factions were the outcome of the disturbance: the blacks and the mulattoes. General Toussaint increased the confusion and instigated the blacks to the severest measures against the colored men. He provoked the conflict and inspired hatred in the heart of both parties."

Toussaint Louverture was nevertheless appointed commandant of the Western province.

General Rochambeau, who stopped at Cap-Français on his way to Santo Domingo, did not approve of all the doings of the Agents; the corruption of the officials was what he censured most severely. He was summarily dismissed by Sonthonax and sent back to France.

While all these intrigues were taking place, the presence of the English seemed to have been entirely forgotten. As a matter of fact they made no effort to avail themselves of the division existing among their opponents.

On June 14, 1796, the Spaniards evacuated Fort Dauphin, which Laveaux occupied; its name was changed to Fort Liberté, which it still retains.

Rochambeau having been deported, there remained but three major-generals in the colony: Laveaux, Commander-in-Chief; Desfourneaux, and Toussaint Louverture. Should Laveaux also be sent off the island, Toussaint would in all probability succeed him, Desfourneaux being already in disfavor. And if only the same could be done to Sonthonax, then would the black general have before him the possibility of attaining the position of highest authority. To obtain this result, Toussaint resorted to a clever device. For the election of the Deputies to the French Legislative Assembly the Agents had summoned to Cap-Français one electoral college only. Up to that time each of the three provinces, North, South and West, had had its electoral assembly. By ordering the electoral college to meet at Cap-Français the Agents thought that it would be a very simple matter to secure the election of men devoted to their party. But they were wrong in their calculations. From Gonaives, where he resided, Toussaint Louverture was able, through the intermediary of Henri Christophe, a member of the electoral college, to rule the elections; he managed to secure the election of Sonthonax and Laveaux, whose removal from Saint-Domingue was indispensable to the realization of his plans. With much delight at having been elected, Laveaux sailed for France on October 19, 1796. Sonthonax, surprised and highly flattered by the honor conferred on him, saw at first in his election but a new token of the devotion of Toussaint Louverture and of the blacks in general.

However, he did not seem to be anxious to leave Saint-Domingue, where he was exercising an absolute dictatorship. His colleague, Giraud, disgusted by all the intrigues which were going on in the island, returned to France. He was soon followed by Leblanc, who sailed on the frigate *La Sémillante*, after having quarrelled with Sonthonax, whom he charged with having tried to poison him: which proves how small was the trust reposed in Sonthonax by his colleagues.

The Agency of the Directory was then reduced to two members: Sonthonax and Julien Raymond, the latter but a negligible quantity. At the end of November, 1796, the news reached Cap-Français that the rank of major-general conferred on Toussaint had been ratified. At the same time the Directory sent to the new major-general a sword and pistol of honor.

Sonthonax, convinced that these demonstrations of his good will had entirely won over Toussaint Louverture, expected that the latter would be henceforth his tool. Relying on his assistance he adopted, on December 13, 1796, a decree ordering the trial of André Rigaud by the Directory and the Legislative Assembly. Without dismissing this general, the decree aimed at curtailing his authority. A. Chanlatte, Beauvais, and Martial Besse were respectively appointed commandants of the arrondissements of Jacmel, Léogane, and Saint-Louis. All of these officers were mulattoes; therefore it was believed that they would become interested in the downfall of André Rigaud, whilst the latter would distrust them: hence would arise fresh discord and the weakening of the power of this class of men. Sonthonax's scheme was a clever one. The Agency declared besides that it would no longer correspond with André Rigaud. To the decree laying the whole Southern province under an interdict the municipality of Cayes responded by authorizing Rigaud to continue in office. And popular manifestations at Jacmel and Saint-Louis prevented Chanlatte and Martial Besse from entering upon their new duties.

The rupture between Sonthonax and Rigaud was complete. It was no difficult matter for Toussaint Louverture to profit by the existing state of things. Being on bad terms with the mulattoes, Sonthonax depended now entirely on him. Toussaint had sided with Laveaux against Villate, because at that time the latter was in his way. But just now he desired to have the support or, at any rate, the neutrality of all classes in order to attain his goal. Therefore it was that though in opposition to Sonthonax's wish he was favorable in his reception of Rigaud's overtures. The friendly relations which resulted between the black and mulatto generals caused grave apprehensions to Sonthonax. It was evident that his enemies were not Toussaint's; and it did not seem as though Rigaud was jealous of the black man who, by his rank of major-general, had become his official superior. In the opinion of the Agent of the Directory, the intimate union of those two men—both all-powerful, one in the South, the other in the North and the West—could only be fraught with great danger for the authority of France. Consequently, no means were to be spared in order to divide them and to provoke bitter enmity against each other, which could only end in strife.

For the time being, Toussaint, by gaining Rigaud's favor, isolated Sonthonax entirely. He also took the precaution of surrounding himself with officers on whose fidelity he could rely.

J. J. Dessalines was in command at Saint Michel, Moise at Dondon, Clervaux at Gonaives, Henri Christophe at Petite-Rivière.

Sonthonax did not even take the trouble of keeping on good terms with General Desfourneaux, whose support, however, might prove useful to him. The latter had displeased him, therefore he decided to get rid of him. To bring about this result he had recourse to Toussaint, who had the greatest interest in the removal of the only officer of equal rank with him. The black general arrived at Cap-Français on the 15th of May, 1797; at night

Desfourneaux was arrested and carried on board. Henceforth Toussaint was the only major-general residing in the colony. On the 3d of May Sonthonax appointed him Commander-in-Chief of the Army of Saint-Domingue.

Yet Toussaint had not helped to annihilate Villate's influence in the North; neither had he succeeded in turning Laveaux out of Saint-Domingue, with the idea of becoming subordinate to Sonthonax. Invested with the highest military authority, his ambition was to succeed Sonthonax as he had already succeeded Laveaux. Meanwhile, he felt the necessity of increasing his prestige; so he started on a campaign against the English. He was successful in expelling them from Vérettes and Mirebalais, but he failed in his attack against Saint-Marc.

In the South, Rigaud, true to France in spite of the decree adopted by Sonthonax, had also renewed hostilities against the English. He could not storm Les Irois, but he succeeded in destroying Dalmarie. The English tried once more to win him over to their cause. Writing to him through Lapointe, they endeavored to speculate upon his supposed jealousy of Toussaint Louverture on account of his being appointed Commander-in-Chief of the army. In his reply Rigaud asserted his devotion to France and defended Toussaint. "I must," said he, "repress your insolence and your insulting tone toward the French General Toussaint Louverture. You have no right to speak of him as a coward, since you do not dare to encounter him; or as a slave, because a French Republican cannot be a slave. His black skin makes no difference between him and his fellow-citizens under a constitution which does not bestow dignities according to one's color."

In spite of Sonthonax's intrigues, Toussaint and Rigaud were then still united. The Commander-in-Chief deemed it time for the realization of his plans. After his defeat before Saint-Marc, his soldiers, who were quite destitute, became somewhat unmanageable. He availed himself of this opportunity to complain of the destitution to which his army had been reduced.

Sonthonax felt that all the responsibility for the sufferings endured by the soldiers was cast upon him. Yet he was unable to remedy the ill effects of the bad management of the finances. In the mean time, he had ordered the arrest of General Pierre-Michel. This arrest, preceded by the arrest of Rochambeau and Desfourneaux, without mentioning the attempt to dismiss Rigaud, made it clear to Toussaint that Sonthonax was not over-scrupulous in getting rid of those who stood in his way or who could no longer be of use to him. Sooner or later his turn would come. Besides, should an intelligent administration not soon find the means of providing for their wants, the soldiers, it was to be feared, would rebel. Toussaint was conscious of the power he possessed and he was confident of being able so successfully to manage the finances as to bring back the former easy circumstances.

On August 15, 1797, he suddenly appeared at Cap-Français. On the 20th he reviewed the troops and secured the good will of the officers. He went afterward to Sonthonax. Accosting the Agent with the greatest deference he handed him a letter inviting him, in the interest of the colony, to go to France and take his seat in the Legislative Assembly. Such a request was equivalent to an order. Sonthonax tried to resist. But he had by his own fault lost the sympathy of those whose assistance might have been of use to him. He had not an influential man, not a competent officer to help him in opposing Toussaint. The latter, noticing the inclination of the Agent to adopt an attitude of firmness, withdrew to Petite Anse, where Henri Christophe was in command. At night on August 23 he fired the alarm-gun. Sonthonax understood the warning and decided to sail. He gave way to Toussaint by leaving Cap-Français on August 25, 1797. The Commander-in-Chief despatched Colonel Vincent to France with the mission of explaining his conduct to the Directory, and he charged Sonthonax with having attempted to induce him to proclaim the independence of Saint-Domingue, making use in this way of the same method to which the Agent had resorted against Rigaud. Moreover, Toussaint believed that the French Government would surely be indulgent to him if he succeeded in expelling the English from the colony. In consequence he reorganized his army, and announced his intention of marching against the invaders. Alexandre Pétion stormed the fortifications of La Coupe built by the English, compelling the latter to retreat to Port-au-Prince. Rigaud, in compliance with Toussaint's order, attacked and took possession of Camp Thomas, not far from Pestel. The campaign was then resumed in the West and in the South.

The Directory now began to be uneasy as to the extent of Toussaint's ambition. But, until the conclusion of peace would allow of their sending sufficient forces to help in restoring the supremacy of the whites, they thought it advisable to be careful in their dealings with the black general. Without openly blaming his actions toward Sonthonax, the Directory sent out General Hédouville to Saint-Domingue. The new Agent arrived at Cap-Français on April 20, 1798. His reception was not enthusiastic on the part of the Commander-in-

Chief, whose desire was to be supreme in command; for this reason he had sent Laveaux and Sonthonax away from the colony. Therefore, it was against all his speculations to be relegated to the second rank just at a time when the success of his campaign against the English left no doubt as to their early expulsion from the island.

In fact, it so happened that a few days after Hédouville's arrival, General Maitland, who was in command of the English forces and whose resources were quite exhausted, wrote to Toussaint Louverture offering to evacuate Port-au-Prince, Arcahaie, and Saint-Marc. The Commander-in-Chief of the army of Saint-Domingue took possession of Saint-Marc on May 8, 1798, of l'Arcahaie on May 12, and of La Croix-des-Bouquets on the 14th. On the 15th he made a triumphal entrance into Port-au-Prince. "The colonists gave him a gorgeous reception. The priests went to meet him with the banners of the church unfurled. They carried the cross and the canopy, as it was the custom at the reception of the Governors-General of Saint-Domingue.

Magnificently dressed white women showered flowers on him. Some colonists even prostrated themselves before him."

White women, who not long ago had regarded the Africans and their descendants with the utmost contempt, were throwing flowers to a former slave! The proud colonists were at the feet of a black man!

Toussaint Louverture had become the protector of the former wealthy planters of Saint-Domingue. Foreseeing the assistance they might be to him he spared nothing in order to secure their good will. Most of the colonists and the emigrants were in the English army. In direct disobedience to the instructions of the representatives of the Directory he granted amnesty to them. From the pulpit he promised them forgiveness; for Toussaint was in the habit of making his speeches or his important declarations from the pulpit of the church. The priests gave him their support and he caused public worship to be observed. Whilst in France religion was being persecuted, in Saint-Domingue the Commander-in-Chief had opened the churches, and after every victory he would be present at a Te Deum in thanksgiving. He rapidly became influential among the whites, to the detriment of Hédouville's prestige. The latter, through obedience to the instructions received from the Directory, appeared to be merciless; he was obliged to put into execution laws enacted against the emigrants, whilst Toussaint was sheltering not only those who were already in Saint-Domingue but also those who continued to arrive in the island.

If the Commander-in-Chief did his utmost to embarrass Hédouville, the latter had no regard for the feelings of the man who was already master of the colony. The young officers recently arrived from France were allowed to make improper remarks concerning the black General; they ridiculed his garb, his religious tendencies. Hédouville boasted that he had the power to dismiss Toussaint from his rank of Commander-in-Chief of the army. The report of all this boasting and malicious criticism angered Toussaint, who already was not too well disposed toward the Agent of the Directory.

Matters soon came to a climax. Rigaud, who still gladly obeyed Toussaint's orders, went to Port-au-Prince in July, 1798, in order to confer with the Commander-in-Chief about a plan of a campaign against Jérémie. The Southern General had defeated the English at Cavaillon and Tiburon. Toussaint and Rigaud left together for Cap-Français, where Hédouville, pleased at having the opportunity of mortifying Toussaint and of exciting his jealousy, gave a most flattering welcome to the mulatto General. True to the policy of the French Government advocating division and discord, the Agent of the Directory managed in this way to sow in the hearts of two gallant officers seeds of hatred which would cause the soil of Saint-Domingue to be once more stained with blood.

However, Toussaint continued in the performance of his duty. He was successful in his negotiations for the evacuation of Jérémie, of which place Rigaud took possession on August 20, 1798. Through his special agent, Huin, the Commander-in-Chief signed with Colonel Harcourt, the representative of General Maitland, a convention for the abandonment of Môle, the last place then occupied by the English (August 16). Almost at the same time (August 18) Dalton, Hédouville's agent at Môle, had come to an agreement with Colonel Stewart for the evacuation of the same place. General Maitland discarded the last agreement and Hédouville's agent was even kept for a while on the *Abergavenny*, then in the harbor of Môle. Anxious to separate from France the man who was omnipotent in Saint-Domingue, the English were exceedingly deferential toward Toussaint. And when, on October 2, 1798, he took possession of Môle, he was received with much state. General Maitland presented him with valuable guns and a bronze culverin. The English General went so far as to suggest that Toussaint should proclaim himself King, promising the assistance of the fleet to protect him in case of need, provided that Great Britain be granted the exclusive privilege of trading

116

with the island. Toussaint's sound common sense put him on his guard against such a proposal. He refused the crown but deemed it wise to maintain good relations with those he had just expelled from the country.

So, after a partial occupation of five years, the English were compelled to quit Saint-Domingue. The island was forever lost to them.

The expulsion of the English was unquestionably due to the successful effort of Toussaint Louverture in the North and in the West, and of Rigaud in the South. The native soldiers, blacks and mulattoes, had had to bear the whole burden of the defense of the colony, the mother country being at that time unable to lend any assistance. As a reward to these brave officers and soldiers, France would soon arm brother against brother by enkindling a criminal war; she would allow Toussaint to crush Rigaud, and would overthrow Toussaint herself; she would even endeavor to restore slavery in Saint-Domingue.

Meanwhile, Hédouville could not conceal his displeasure at Toussaint's actions. On September 5, 1798, he wrote to the Commander-in-Chief as follows: "I would congratulate you about the reception given you by General Maitland, were I not convinced that you are the dupe of his perfidy; you dared to write to me that you have more confidence in him than in me. What is the meaning of the great number of emigrants who flock to our shores on English cartel-ships? You would do well to remember the orders and instructions I transmitted to you, and you may rest assured that I intend that they shall be obeyed." At the same time the Agent of the Directory declared void the amnesty which had been granted at Port-au-Prince to the emigrants by Toussaint; he also blamed the municipality for having officially attended a religious ceremony. However, in a proclamation on October 10, 1798, in which he recalled the success achieved against the English, the Commander-in-Chief ordered what follows: "Morning and evening prayers be said by the soldiers and that the generals would cause a Te Deum to be celebrated to return thanks to God for the success of the army and for the return to the colony of thousands of emigrants."

Whilst Toussaint Louverture was offering thanksgiving for the return to the colony of thousands of emigrants, Hédouville, on October 14, renewed his order prohibiting the admission into Saint-Domingue of these same emigrants. The conflict between the two generals was assuming an alarming aspect. Several officers under Toussaint's command had already begun to disregard Hédouville's authority. Dessalines, who was Commandant of the Arrondissement of Saint-Marc, had flatly refused to carry out one of his orders. Moise, Commandant of the Arrondissement of Fort Liberté, assumed such a threatening attitude that the representative of the French Government decided to dismiss him. But Toussaint Louverture's nephew, who was fully aware of his uncle's intentions, warned the people to be prepared for all contingencies.

Hédouville, still believing that he could assert his authority, invested Manigat, a justice of the peace at Fort Liberté, with all the civil and military powers. In order to prevent any disturbance of the peace the magistrate ordered the disarmament of the Fifth Regiment. A bloody fight ensued; and Moise, fearing to be arrested, fled to the country, where he set to work to stir up the people (October 16, 1798). A band of armed peasants marched to Cap-Français, where they were joined by Dessalines. Like Sonthonax, Hédouville was then compelled to leave Saint-Domingue. He sailed on October 23, 1798, on the frigate *La Bravoure*. In a proclamation issued the day before he had censured Toussaint Louverture's behavior in very strong terms. And, in order to divide the blanks and mulattoes, he had authorized Rigaud to defy the authority of the Commander-in-Chief of the Army. On October 22 he wrote as follows to the Commandant of the Southern province: "Compelled to quit the colony through the ambition and perfidy of General Toussaint Louverture, who has sold himself to the English, the emigrants, and the Americans,—and has violated his most solemn oaths,—I release *you entirely from the authority intrusted to him as a Commander-in-Chief*, and I entreat you to assume the command of the Southern Département as designated in the law of Brumaire 4th ..."

After the sailing of the representative of France, Toussaint went to Cap-Français, where, in accordance with his habits, he ordered the singing of the Te Deum. He set in motion all the communes of the colony; and they sent to him numerous addresses protesting against Hédouville's behavior. He gave over all these addresses to Gaze, whom he despatched to France to explain to the Directory the recent occurrences in Saint-Domingue. And in order to disclaim the appearance of all pretensions to independence, he hastened to ask Roume, who was at Santo Domingo, to come and reside in the French portion of the island. Meanwhile, he did not conceal his resentment at Hédouville's letter to Rigaud. He quite naturally believed that the Commandant of the Southern province was in full sympathy with the Agent of France. This started a bitter exchange of letters between the two principal military authorities of the colony. Conceit and false pride played a large part in aggravating the disagreement between the two generals.

Rigaud enjoyed great prestige in the South. Released by Hédouville's order from all obedience to Toussaint, and thus rendered somewhat independent, there was a possibility of his becoming a dangerous rival. To maintain his authority it would be necessary for Toussaint completely to cripple the power of the only man who could successfully resist him. Therefore he lost no time in beginning to discredit him.

Such was the situation when, on January 12, 1799, Roume arrived at Port-au-Prince. After concerting with Toussaint Louverture he called a meeting of Rigaud, Beauvais, and Laplume. At this meeting, which took place at Port-au-Prince, Roume requested Rigaud to resign his position of Commander-in-Chief of the Southern province and to relinquish Petit-Goave and Grand-Goave to Laplume, who was already in command of the Arrondissement of Léogane. By accepting such a proposal Rigaud's authority would have been reduced to nothing practically. So he tendered a full resignation of all his authority; and having been elected Deputy to the Legislative Assembly, he asked Roume to allow him to go to France and take his seat in that body.

The departure of Rigaud would have removed many difficulties; it would have satisfied Toussaint's ambition for the time being; all power would be his in the colony. All cause of conflict between the natives of Saint-Domingue would thus have disappeared. Knowing as he did the misunderstanding which, since Hédouville's letter, existed between Toussaint and Rigaud, Roume was in duty bound to accept the latter 's resignation. However, he refused it. The policy of France aimed at that time to divide the blacks and the mulattoes in order to be able to restore the supremacy of the whites by subduing each of them individually. Roume, who was cognizant of the ulterior designs of the Directory, was determined to do his utmost to provoke and keep up the mistrust existing between the two parties. He persisted in refusing to accept the resignation which Rigaud again made to him, and he succeeded in deciding him not only to remain in Saint-Domingue but also caused a weakening of his authority by transferring the command of Grand-Goave and Petit-Goave to Laplume. This arrangement did not meet with Toussaint Louverture's full approval, as it still left his rival with a great deal of influence, whereas it was his wish to get him out of the colony. To bring about this end, he determined to avail himself of the first opportunity to make a rupture inevitable. As the consequence of a riot which occurred at Corail, thirty of the malcontents, twenty-nine of whom were black and one white, were imprisoned in the jail of Jérémie; they died from asphyxiation. Whilst this was taking place Rigaud was at Petit-Goave, on his way to Cayes. Upon learning of this unfortunate occurrence Toussaint Louverture, then in Port-au-Prince (February 21, 1799), treated it as a matter of the greatest importance. The drummers went through the streets beating "La Générale"; the whole population was summoned to the cathedral. From the pulpit Toussaint denounced Rigaud as the enemy of the blacks and afterward wrote him a most insulting letter.

Roume purposely held aloof and allowed the quarrel to grow more bitter. Since February 25 he had left for Cap-Français; but he continued to keep up a cordial correspondence with the Commandant of the Southern province. However, he suddenly issued a proclamation in which he denounced Rigaud as a man whose ambition was a menace to the established governmental authority.

Nevertheless, Roume did not dismiss him, neither did he inflict on him any disciplinary measure. Instead of this he requested Toussaint Louverture to call the insubordinate to order, thus attaining his end in creating a civil war.

Rigaud found himself in a sad dilemma: he had to choose between fighting or fleeing from Saint-Domingue. He accepted the former alternative—incited by his hasty temper, the recollection of his past services to France and the authority intrusted to him, which he considered his duty to exercise. Toussaint proceeded with his usual caution in preparing for the unavoidable struggle by taking such measures as to insure him success. He gave special thought to the supplies of his army, provisions being somewhat scarce. For this reason lie entered into direct relations with John Adams, then the President of the United States, who appointed Edward Stevens Consul-General at Saint-Domingue. Toussaint's negotiations with England and the United States resulted in a similar commercial arrangement with both countries, to which Roume gave his approval in April, 1799. The two powers pledged their assistance to the black General. In consequence General Maitland advised his agents to give their unreserved support to Toussaint and to do their utmost to prevent a reconciliation between the latter and Rigaud, whilst President Adams placed under an interdict all the southern ports of Saint-Domingue, and by a proclamation of June 26, 1799, prohibited their entrance to all American ships, thus depriving Rigaud of the means of getting provisions and war material. He even went so far as to place American men-of-war at the disposal of Toussaint, so much was he won over to the latter's cause.

The conflict brought about by the intrigues of the Agents of France broke out at last. At night on the 17th of June, 1799, Rigaud's soldiers who were quartered at Pont-de-Miragoane attacked and stormed the fort of Petit-Goave. Bloodshed had started; men were about to kill their own brothers, and all to the greatest satisfaction of the colonists, who saw visions of reconquering their former influence through this great sacrifice of human life. Toussaint displayed his usual activity. After repressing a rebellion at Môle Saint-Nicolas he centred his efforts against Jacmel, which was being besieged by General Dessalines, Commander-in-Chief of the forces in the South. The few ships used in the blockade of the town were inadequate to prevent the landing of supplies of provisions sent to the besieged town. Toussaint then claimed the promised assistance of President John Adams, as a result of which a brig and a frigate of the United States Navy cruised before Jacmel and chased away the small crafts which were endeavoring to revictual the town.

The besieged people of Jacmel had been successively deserted by their leaders Beauvais and Birot; however, they kept up a valiant defense under the command of Pétion, who at the eleventh hour had come to their help. Being unable any longer to resist the famine and the consequent diseases arising from it, they evacuated the town on March 10, 1800. The fall of Jacmel was the beginning of the overthrow of Rigaud. In spite of their great bravery his soldiers could not check the steady advance of Toussaint's more powerful army. On July 28, 1800, Dessalines was at a distance of only three leagues from Cayes, the port of which was blockaded by two frigates and two schooners of the United States Navy. Rigaud's cause was irretrievably lost. Flight was the only course open to him; consequently, he left Cayes and sailed from Tiburon on July 29, 1800, on a Danish ship bound for Saint Thomas.

The 1st of August, 1800, Toussaint Louverture arrived at Cayes. According to his custom he went to the church, where, after the usual Te Deum had been chanted, he ascended the pulpit and proclaimed a full oblivion of all the happenings of the past. For some time to come Saint-Domingue knew no other master. Toussaint had supreme command. He had meantime unfortunately lost the sympathy and devotion of many friends: a fact which he would have bitter cause to regret in the short space of two years after his glorious triumph.

Concise view of the History of Toussaint Louverture and Haitian Revolutions [3]

Instead of one, as is usually believed, there were three distinct revolutions in the island during the fourteen years which elapsed from 1789 to 1803. The first revolution was for the establishment of republican principles, and was confined to the whites. The second revolution established the emancipation of the slaves. The third revolution achieved the independence of the colony from the mother country, and was not completed until ten years afterwards, 1802.

The intervening time was distinguished by a series of events over which Toussaint Louverture became the presiding genius.

In estimating the character of Toussaint Louverture, regard must be paid, not to the enlightened age in which he lived, but to the rank in society from which he sprang — a rank which must be classed with a remote and elementary age of mankind.

---

[3] Based on the Speech of James McCune Smith

Born forty-seven years before the commencement of the revolt, he had reached the prime of manhood, a slave, with a soul uncontaminated by the degradation which surrounded him. Living in a state of society where worse than polygamy was actually urged, we find him at this period faithful to one wife — the wife of his youth — and the father of an interesting family. Linked with such tender ties, and enlightened with some degree of education, which his indulgent master, M. Bayou, had given him, he fulfilled, up to the moment of the revolt, the duties of a Christian man in slavery.

At the time of the insurrection—in which he took no part — he continued in the peaceable discharge of his duties as coachman; and when the insurgents approached the estate whereon he lived, he accomplished the flight of M. Bayou, whose kind treatment (part of this kindness was teaching this slave to read and write) he repaid by forwarding to him produce for his maintenance while in exile in these United States.

Having thus faithfully acquitted himself as a slave, he turned towards the higher destinies which awaited him as a freeman. With a mind stored with patient reflection upon the biographies of men, the most eminent in civil and military affairs; and deeply versed in the history of the most remarkable revolutions that had yet occurred amongst mankind, he entered the army of the insurgents under Jean François. This chief rapidly promoted him to the offices of physician to the forces, aid-de-camp, and colonel. Jean François, in alliance with the Spaniards, maintained war at this time for the cause of royalty.

Whilst serving under this chief, Toussaint beheld another civil war agitating the French colony. On one side, the French Commissioners, who had acknowledged the emancipation of the slaves, maintained war for the Republic; on the other side, the old noblesse, or planters, fought under the royal banner, having called in the aid of the British forces in order to re-establish slavery and the ancient regime.

In this conflict, unmindful of their solemn oaths against the decree of the 15th of May, 1791, the whites of both parties, including the planters, hesitated not to fight in the same ranks, shoulder to shoulder, with the blacks. Caste was forgotten in the struggle for principles!

At this juncture Jean François, accompanied by his principal officers, and possessed of all the honors and emoluments of a captain-general in the service of his Catholic Majesty, retired to Spain, leaving Toussaint at liberty to choose his party. Almost immediately joining that standard which acknowledged and battled for equal rights to all men, he soon rendered signal service to the Commissioners, by driving the Spaniards from the northern, and by holding the British at bay in the eastern part of the island. For these services he was raised to the rank of general by the French commander at Porte-aux-Paix, General Laveaux, a promotion which he soon repaid by saving that veteran's life under the following circumstances: Villate, a mulatto general, envious of the honors bestowed on Toussaint, treacherously imprisoned General Laveaux in Cape François. Immediately upon hearing this fact, Toussaint hastened to the Cape at the head of 10,000 men and liberated his benefactor. And, at the very moment of his liberation, a commission arrived from France appointing General Laveaux Governor of the Colony; his first official act was to proclaim Toussaint his lieutenant. "This is the black," said Laveaux, "predicted by Raynal, and who is destined to avenge the outrages committed against his whole race." A remark soon verified, for on his attainment of the supreme power, Toussaint avenged those injuries — by forgiveness!

As an acknowledgment for his eminent services against the British, and against the mulattoes, who, inflamed with all the bitterness of *caste*, had maintained a sanguinary war under their great leader Rigaud, in the southern part of the colony, the Commissioners invested Toussaint with the office and dignity of general-in-chief of Santo Domingo.

From that moment began the full development of the vast and versatile genius of this extraordinary man. Standing amid the terrible, because hostile, fragments of two revolutions, harassed by the rapacious greed of commissioners upon commissioners, who, successively dispatched from France, hid beneath a republican exterior a longing after the spoils; with an army in the field accustomed by five years' experience to all the license of civil war, Toussaint, with a giant hand, seized the reins of government, reduced these conflicting elements to harmony and order, and raised the colony to nearly its former prosperity, his lofty intellect always delighting to effect its object rather by the tangled mazes of diplomacy than by the strong arm of physical force, yet maintaining a steadfast and unimpeached adherence to truth, his word, and his honor.

General Maitland, commander of the British forces, finding the reduction of the island to be utterly hopeless, signed a treaty with Toussaint for the evacuation of all the posts which he held. "Toussaint then paid him a visit, and was received with military honors. After partaking of a grand entertainment, he was presented by General Maitland, in the name of His Majesty, with a splendid service of plate, and put in possession of the government-house which had been built and furnished by the English."

*

Buonaparte, on becoming First Consul, sent out the confirmation of Toussaint as commander-in-chief, who, with views infinitely beyond the short-sighted and selfish vision of the Commissioners, proclaimed a general amnesty to the planters who had fled during the revolutions, earnestly invited their return to the possession of their estates, and, with a delicate regard to their feelings, decreed that the epithet "emigrant" should not be applied to them. Many of the planters accepted the invitation, and returned to the peaceful possession of their estates.

In regard to the army of Toussaint, General Lacroix, one of the planters who returned, affirms "that never was a European army subjected to a more rigid discipline than that which was observed by the troops of Toussaint." Yet this army was converted by the commander-in-chief into industrious laborers, by the simple expedient of *paying them for their labor.* "When he restored many of the planters to their estates, there was no restoration of their former property in human beings. No human being was to be bought or sold. Severe tasks, flagellations, and scanty food were no longer to be endured. The planters were obliged to employ their laborers on the footing of hired servants." "And under this system," says Lacroix, "the colony advanced, as if by enchantment towards its ancient splendor; cultivation was extended with such rapidity that every day made its progress more perceptible. All appeared to be happy, and regarded Toussaint as their guardian angel. In making a tour of the island, he was hailed by the blacks with universal joy, nor was he less a favorite of the whites."

Toussaint, having effected a bloodless conquest of the Spanish territory, had now become commander of the entire island. Performing all the executive duties, he made laws to suit the exigency of the times. His Egeria was temperance accompanied with a constant activity of body and mind.

The best proof of the entire success of his government is contained in the comparative views of the exports of the island, before the revolutions, and during the administration of Toussaint. Bear in mind that, "before the revolution there were

450,000 slave laborers working with a capital in the shape of buildings, mills, fixtures, and implements, which had been accumulating during a century. Under Toussaint there were 290,000 free laborers, many of them just from the army or the mountains, working on plantations that had undergone the devastation of insurrection and a seven years' war."

*

In consequence of the almost entire cessation of official communication with France, and for other reasons equally good, Toussaint thought it necessary for the public welfare to frame a new constitution for the government of the island. With the aid of M. Pascal, Abbe Moliere, and Marinit, he drew up a constitution, and submitted the same to a General Assembly convened from every district, and by that assembly the constitution was adopted. It was subsequently promulgated in the name of the people. And, on the 1st of July, 1801, the island was declared to be an independent State, in which *all men*, without regard to complexion or creed, possessed *equal rights*.

This proceeding was subsequently sanctioned by Napoleon Buonaparte, whilst First Consul. In a letter to Toussaint, he says, "We have conceived for you esteem, and we wish to recognize and proclaim the great services you have rendered the French people. If their colors fly on Santo Domingo, it is to you and your brave blacks that we owe it. Called by your talents and the force of circumstances to the chief command, you have terminated the civil war, put a stop to the persecutions of some ferocious men, and restored to honor the religion and the worship of God, from whom all things come. The situation in which you were placed, surrounded on all sides by enemies, and without the mother country being able to succor or sustain you, has rendered legitimate the articles of that constitution."

Although Toussaint enforced the duties of religion, he entirely severed the connection between Church and State. He rigidly enforced all the duties of morality, and would not suffer in his presence even the approach to indecency of dress or manner. "Modesty," said he, "is the defense of woman."

The chief, nay the idol of an army of 100,000 well-trained and acclimated troops ready to march or sail where he wist, Toussaint refrained from raising the standard of liberty in any one of the neighboring island, at a time when, had he been fired with what men term ambition, he could easily have revolutionized the entire archipelago of the west. But his thoughts were bent on conquest of another kind; he was determined to overthrow an *error* which designing and interested men had craftily instilled into the civilized world,—a belief in the natural inferiority of the Negro race. It was the glory and the warrantable boast of Toussaint that he had been the instrument of demonstrating that, even with the worst odds against them, this race is entirely capable of achieving liberty and of self-government. He did more: by abolishing caste he proved the artificial nature of such distinctions, and further demonstrated that even slavery cannot unfit men for the full exercise of all the functions which belong to free citizens.

"Some situations of trust were filled by free Negroes and mulattoes, who had been in respectable circumstances under the old Government; but others were occupied by Negroes, and even by Africans, who had recently emerged from the lowest condition of slavery."

But the bright and happy state of things which the genius of Toussaint had almost created out of elements the most discordant was doomed to be of short duration. For the dark spirit of Napoleon, glutted, but not satiated with the glory banquet afforded at the expense of Europe and Africa, seized upon this, the most beautiful and happy of the Hesperides, as the next victim of its remorseless rapacity.

With the double intention of getting rid of the republican army, and reducing back to slavery the island of Haiti, he sent out his brother-in-law, General Leclerc, with 26 ships of war and 25,000 men.

Like Leonidas at Thermopylæ, or the Bruce at Bannockburn, Toussaint determined to defend from thraldom his sea-girt isle, made sacred to liberty by the baptism of blood.

On the 28th of January, 1802, Leclerc arrived off the bay of Samana, from the promontory of which Toussaint, in anxious alarm, beheld for the first time in his life so large an armament. "We must all perish," said he, "all France has come to Saint-Domingue!" But this despondency passed away in a moment, and then this man, who had been a kindly-treated slave, prepared to oppose to the last that system which he now considered worse than death.

It is impossible, after so long a tax on your patience, to enter on a detailed narration of the conflict which ensued. The hour of trial served only to develop and ennoble the character of Toussaint, who rose, with misfortune, above the allurements of rank and wealth which were offered as the price of his submission; and the very ties of parental love he yielded to the loftier sentiment of patriotism.

On the 2nd of February, a division of Leclerc's army, commanded by General Rochambeau, an old planter, landed at Fort Dauphin, and ruthlessly murdered many of the inhabitants (freedmen) who, unarmed, had been led by curiosity to the beach, in order to witness the disembarkation of the troops.

Christophe, one of the generals of Toussaint, commanding at Cape François [Le Cap], having resisted the menaces and the flattery of Leclerc, reduced that ill-fated town to ashes, and retired with his troops into the mountains, carrying with him 2,000 of the white inhabitants of the Cape, who were protected from injury during the fierce war which ensued.

Having full possession of the plain of the Cape, Leclerc, with a proclamation of liberty in his hand, in March following re-established slavery with all its former cruelties.

This treacherous movement thickened the ranks of Toussaint, who thenceforward so vigorously pressed his opponent, that as a last resort, Leclerc broke the shackles of the slave, and proclaimed "Liberty and equality to all the inhabitants of Santo Domingo."

This proclamation terminated the conflict for the time. Christophe and Dessalines, general officers, and at length Toussaint himself, capitulated, and, giving up the command of the island to Leclerc, he retired, at the suggestion of that officer, to enjoy rest and the sweet endearments of his family circle, on one of his estates near Gonaives. At this place he had remained about one month, when, without any adequate cause, Leclerc caused him to be seized, and to be placed on board of a ship of war, in which he was conveyed to France, where, without trial or condemnation, he was imprisoned in a loathsome and unhealthy dungeon. Unaccustomed to the chill and damp of this prison-house, the aged frame of Toussaint gave way, and he died.

In this meagre outline of his life I have presented simply facts, gleaned, for the most part, from the unwilling testimony of his foes, and therefore resting on good authority. The highest encomium on his character is contained in the fact that Napoleon believed that by capturing him he would be able to re-enslave Haiti; and even this encomium is, if possible, rendered higher by the circumstances which afterward transpired, which showed that his principles were so thoroughly disseminated among his brethren, that, without the presence of Toussaint, they achieved that liberty which he had taught them so rightly to estimate.

The capture of Toussaint spread like wild-fire through the island, and his principal officers again took the field. A fierce and sanguinary war ensued, in which the French gratuitously inflicted the most awful cruelties on their prisoners, many of whom having been hunted with bloodhounds, were carried in ships to some distance from the shore, murdered in cold blood, and cast into the sea; their corpses were thrown by the waves back upon the beach, and filled the air with pestilence, by which the French troops perished in large numbers. Leclerc having perished by pestilence, his successor, Rochambeau, when the conquest of the island was beyond possibility, became the cruel perpetrator of these bloody deeds.

Thus it will be perceived that treachery and massacre were begun on the side of the French. I place emphasis on these facts in order to endeavor to disabuse the public mind of an attempt to attribute to emancipation the acts of retaliation resorted to by the Haitians in *imitation* of what the enlightened French had taught them. In two daily papers of this city there were published, a year since, a series of articles entitled the "Massacres of Santo Domingo."

The "massacres" are not attributable to emancipation, for we have proved otherwise in regard to the first of them. The other occurred in 1804, twelve years after the slaves had disenthralled themselves. Fearful as the latter may have been, it did not equal the atrocities previously committed on the Haitians by the French. And the massacre was restricted to the white French inhabitants, whom Dessalines, the Robespierre of the island, suspected of an attempt to bring back slavery, with the aid of a French force yet hovering in the neighborhood.

And if we search for the cause of this massacre, we may trace   it to the following source: Nations which are pleased to term themselves civilized have one sort of faith which they hold to one another, and another sort which they entertain towards people less advanced in refinement. The faith which they entertain towards the latter is, very often, treachery, in the vocabulary of the civilized. It was treachery towards Toussaint that caused the massacre of Santo Domingo; it was treachery towards Osceola that brought bloodhounds into Florida!

General Rochambeau, with the remnant of the French army, having been reduced to the dread necessity of striving "to appease the calls of hunger by feeding on horses, mules, and the very dogs that had been employed in hunting down and devouring the Negroes," evacuated the island in the autumn of 1803, and Haiti thenceforward became an independent State.

This presentation is a concise view of the revolutions of Haiti in the relation of cause and effect.

www.ingramcontent.com/pod-product-compliance
Lightning Source LLC
Chambersburg PA
CBHW031320040426
42443CB00005B/154